WISSEN & TESTEN

Englisch

Grammatik

8.–10. Klasse

W0345964

WISSEN & TESTEN

Englisch
8.–10. Klasse

Grammatik

Cornelsen
SCRIPTOR

Autor dieses Bandes:
David Clarke ist Brite. Nach langjähriger Tätigkeit als Englischlehrer an deutschen Schulen arbeitet er jetzt als Schulbuchautor. Er hat zahlreiche Lehrwerke und Übungsmaterialien veröffentlicht.

www.cornelsen.de

Bibliografische Information: Die Deutsche Bibliothek verzeichnet diese Publikation in der Deutschen Nationalbibliografie; detaillierte bibliografische Daten sind im Internet über http://dnb.ddb.de abrufbar.

Dieser Band folgt den Regeln der deutschen Rechtschreibung, die seit August 2006 gelten.

5.	4.	3.	2.	1.	Die letzten Ziffern bezeichnen
13	12	11	10	09	Zahl und Jahr der Auflage.

© 2009 Cornelsen Verlag Scriptor GmbH & Co. KG, Berlin
Das Werk und seine Teile sind urheberrechtlich geschützt. Jede Nutzung in anderen als den gesetzlich zugelassenen Fällen bedarf deshalb der vorherigen schriftlichen Einwilligung des Verlags.
Hinweis zu den §§ 46, 52a UrhG: Weder das Werk noch seine Teile dürfen ohne eine solche Einwilligung eingescannt und in ein Netzwerk gestellt oder sonst öffentlich zugänglich gemacht werden. Dies gilt auch für Intranets von Schulen und sonstigen Bildungseinrichtungen.
Redaktion: Marion Clausen, Göttingen
Reihen- und Gesamtgestaltung: Dagmar & Torsten Lemme, Berlin
Druck und Bindearbeiten: CPI – Clausen & Bosse, Leck
Printed in Germany
ISBN 978-3-589-22768-6

Gedruckt auf säurefreiem Papier,
umweltschonend hergestellt aus chlorfrei gebleichten Faserstoffen.

Vorwort

Liebe Schülerin, lieber Schüler!

Die neue Reihe ***WISSEN & TESTEN*** informiert dich knapp und genau über das Wichtigste aus einem Fach.

In übersichtlichen Lerneinheiten bekommst du auf den WISSEN-Seiten leicht verständliche Erklärungen, Regeln und Beispiele zu einem Thema. Auf den anschließenden Seiten zum TESTEN kannst du sofort überprüfen, ob du alles verstanden hast. Hier findest du Fragen und Übungen, die genau zu den vorigen Seiten passen.
Am Ende jeder Einheit stehen die Lösungen auf einem gesonderten Farbfeld, sodass du gleich kontrollieren kannst, ob du alles richtig gemacht hast. Jede Lerneinheit umfasst eine oder zwei Doppelseiten.
Im Inhaltsverzeichnis findest du schnell die Themen, die du gerade üben willst.

WISSEN & TESTEN Englisch Grammatik erklärt alles Wichtige, was du im Englischunterricht brauchst und veranschaulicht es durch viele Beispiele.

Im Anhang findest du außerdem zum Nachschlagen die Übersichten über:

- Präpositionen
- Verben mit Adverbien oder Präpositionen
- unregelmäßige Verben
- englische Wendungen
- „Falsche Freunde“

Mit diesem Buch kannst du dein Wissen auffrischen, dir Hilfe für Hausaufgaben oder Referate holen und testen, ob du fit für die nächste schriftliche Prüfung bist.

Viel Erfolg!

Inhalt

Wortarten

Das Verb

Satzgefüge

Satzarten

Anhang

1

Die Nomen

Personen- und sachbezogene Nomen

Anders als im Deutschen gibt es im Englischen nur ein **„natürliches"** – also kein „grammatisches" – **Geschlecht.** Nomen wie *girl, mother, woman* usw. beziehen sich auf weibliche Personen; Nomen wie *boy, father, man* usw. auf männliche.

The girl** told **her father** about **the accident.

Die meisten **personenbezogenen Nomen** – z. B. *cyclist, doctor, driver, friend, teacher* usw. – können sich aber auf weibliche und männliche Personen beziehen. In solchen Fällen wird das Geschlecht der Person nur durch Pronomen wie *he, she, his, her* usw. oder durch Eigennamen deutlich.

A cyclist** crossed **the road** in front of **a car.
***The car driver** stopped in time and so **she** didn't hit the cyclist.*
*But the cyclist fell off **his bike** and hurt **his hand.***

Einige **berufsbezogene Nomen** haben eine geschlechtsbezogene Form, z. B. *actor – actress, waiter – waitress, policeman – policewoman, headmaster – headmistress.* Sie kommen aber viel seltener im Englischen als im Deutschen vor.

***A policeman** came and called a doctor.*

Im Englischen haben **Dinge** kein Geschlecht: *the accident* (der Unfall), *the road* (die Straße), *the car* (das Auto), *the bike* (das Rad), *the hand* (die Hand). Für alle Dinge wird das **Pronomen** *it* verwendet.

Tiere sind im Englischen in der Regel sächlich. Bei **Haustieren mit Namen** dagegen benutzen wir, wie bei Menschen, *he* bzw. *she.*

Überprüfe hier, ob das Wissen sitzt

1 Unterstreiche die Nomen.

The phone rang at the school. Ann Bell, the secretary, answered it.

"Good morning," she said. "Can I help you?"

"Yes," said a strange, deep voice at the other end. "I just want to tell you that Mike Davis can't come to lessons today. The doctor says he must stay in bed. He has a bad cold."

"Oh, I'm sorry about that," said Ann, "but don't worry. I'll tell Mike's teachers. But who's speaking, please?"

"My father," said the caller.

2 Vervollständige die Übersetzungen.

a Der Bus war zu spät. Er hatte eine Panne.

The __________ was late. ____________ a breakdown.

b Diese Uhr geht nicht. Sie braucht eine neue Batterie.

This ____________ doesn't work. ________________ a new battery.

c Ich kenne das Mädchen. Es wohnt in meiner Straße.

I know _____________ . _________________ in my street.

d Die Katze gehört meinem Nachbarn. Sie heißt Tiggy.

____________ belongs to my neighbour. __________________ Tiggy.

e Der Film war okay, aber ich fand ihn zu lang.

________________ was okay but I found __________________ .

1 phone – school – secretary – morning – voice – lessons – doctor – bed – cold – teachers – father – caller

2
a bus; It had
b clock; It needs
c the girl; She lives
d The cat; She is called
e The film; it too long

TESTEN • TESTEN • TESTEN • TESTEN • TESTEN • TESTEN • TESTEN

Die regelmäßige und unregelmäßige Pluralbildung

Die regelmäßige Pluralbildung

Bei den meisten Nomen bilden wir den Plural durch das einfache Anhängen eines *-s*.

*At a lot of British **schools, pupils** have eight **lessons** a day, five **days** a week.*

Diese **Schreibregeln** sind zu beachten:
Endet der Singular auf einem Zischlaut, wird *-es* angehängt.
*Most pupils bring **sandwiches** to school in **boxes.***

Endet der Singular auf *-y* nach einem Konsonanten, wird das *-y* zu *-i*. Hinzu kommt *-es*:

family → *families*
baby → *babies*

*There are eight **families** in our house and two of them have **babies.***

Endet der Singular auf *-fe*, wird *-f* zu *-v*. Hinzu kommt *-s*:

life → *lives*
wife → *wives*

*Don't eat with your fingers. Use **knives** and forks.*

Endet der Singular auf *-f*, wird im Plural daraus meist *-ves*:

leaf → *leaves*

Endet der Singular auf *-o*, wird der Plural auf *-s* („leblose Dinge") bzw. *-es* (Menschen, Pflanzen) gebildet:

photo → *photos*
radio → *radios*
video → *videos*
hero → *heroes*
potato → *potatoes*
tomato → *tomatoes*

*You mustn't bring **radios** to school with you.*
*Please buy some **tomatoes** on your way home.*

Die unregelmäßige Pluralbildung

Eine kleine Zahl von Nomen hat einen unregelmäßigen Plural.
Die wichtigsten Formen sind:

child → *children*
man → *men*
woman → *women*
tooth → *teeth*
foot → *feet*
goose → *geese*
mouse → *mice*

*How many **children** have the Greens got?*
***Men** still get more money than **women** for the same job.*
*Always clean your **teeth** after a meal.*

Eine noch kleinere Zahl von Nomen hat **die gleiche Form** im Singular und im Plural:

sheep → *sheep*
fish → *fish*
fruit → *fruit*

*Some say that **sheep** are very stupid animals.*

Überprüfe hier, ob das Wissen sitzt

1 Setze die richtigen Pluralformen in die Sätze ein.

a Young ____________ (child) need lots of ____________ (kiss) and ________ (hug).

b ___________ (Lady) and ________________ (gentleman), tonight I want to talk about the danger to _________ (crop) from farm ________________ (chemical).

c Supermarkets sell ________ (fruit) and __________________ (vegetable) as well as _______ (fish), _________ (meat) and other _______ (food).

d __________________ (Supporter) of fox hunting say that there will be a plague of _________ (fox) if their sport is banned.

e Small children should learn to ride on __________ (pony) or even ___________ (donkey) before they go on to ride _________ (horse).

f The parts of website _________________ (address) are often separated by ________ (dot) and _____________ (slash).

g There are so many ___________ (wolf) in Eastern Europe now that they have begun to attack _________ (sheep), _________ (calf) and even __________ (person).

h Nowadays, advanced ______________ (society) are a jigsaw of ethnic ____________ (minority) and interest ________ (group).

i It's a scandal that in many ___________ (country) ___________ (woman) who stay at home to look after their ___________ (family) do not get ______________ (pension) in old age.

2 Streiche die falsche Form der Nomen durch.

a Is this all the ~~thank~~/thanks *(Dank)* I get for my hard work/works?

b Lindenstraße is one of the most popular German TV serie/series.

c The outskirt/outskirts of most big towns aren't/isn't very attractive.

d We hear a lot about woman's/women's rights, but what about children's/child's rights?

e Nowadays most geese/gooses are imported from Poland and Hungary, aren't they/isn't it?

f You can't get teeth/tooths or glass/glasses free any longer. You have to pay for it/them.

g There are so many deer/deers in the forest that they are damaging the trees.

h Don't sit down, please. Your trouser is/trousers are covered with paint/paints.

i Cow/Cows and ox/oxen, for example, are cattle *(Rindvieh)*. You will find a lot of cattle/cattles on dairy farms.

j The police are/is questioning pupil/pupils about the fire.

k The Swiss/Swisses have four official languages.

1 a children – kisses – hugs
b Ladies – gentlemen – crops – chemicals
c fruit – vegetables – fish – meat – food
d Supporters – foxes
e ponies – donkeys – horses
f addresses – dots – slashes
g wolves – sheep – calves – persons
h societies – minorities – groups
i countries – women – families – pensions

2 a thanks – work
b series
c outskirts – aren't
d women's – children's
e geese – aren't they
f teeth – glasses – them
g deer
h trousers are – paint
i Cows – oxen – cattle
j are – pupils
k Swiss

Zählbare und nichtzählbare Nomen

Nomen wie *apples, bananas* und *eggs* sind **zählbar.** Sie haben eine Pluralform und können mit *a/an* und Zahlwörtern benutzt werden. Daher sagen wir *an/one apple, two apples, three apples* usw.

I'd like ***an apple*** *and* ***a banana****, please.*

Do you want ***one*** *or* ***two eggs*** *for breakfast?*

Nomen wie *milk* und *butter* sind **nichtzählbar.** Sie haben keine Pluralform und können deswegen nicht mit *a/an* oder Zahlwörtern benutzt werden. Wollen wir **nichtzählbare Begriffe im Plural** benutzen, dann müssen wir ein geeignetes zählbares Nomen – z. B. *bottle of* oder *packet of* – hinzufügen.

Please buy ***some milk*** *and* ***some butter.***

Sure. How much do we need?

Three bottles of milk *and* ***two packets of butter*** *will be enough.*

Diese Nomen sind im Englischen **nichtzählbar.** Wie bei allen anderen nichtzählbaren Begriffen haben sie keine Pluralform. Daher stehen die **dazugehörigen Verben und Pronomen** immer im Singular:

advice	Rat, Ratschläge
damage	Schaden, Schäden
evidence	Beweis(e)
furniture	Möbel
hair	Haar
homework	Hausaufgabe(n)
information	Information(en)
knowledge	Wissen, Kenntnis(se)
progress	Fortschritt(e)

Our ***furniture is*** *awful. Just look at* ***it.***

Überprüfe hier, ob das Wissen sitzt

Setze zuerst die Nomen aus Kästchen A in die Tabelle ein. Dann trage die Pluralform der zählbaren Nomen ein. Schließlich füge einen geeigneten Ausdruck aus Kästchen B zu, um die nichtzählbaren Nomen „zählbar“ zu machen.

A box, bread, bus, car, child, chocolate, coffee, evidence, family, glass *(Glas)*, glue, house, knife, meat, oil, woman, wine

B bars of, bottles of, cans of, cups of, loaves of, pieces of, sheets of; slices of, tubes of

Zählbar		Nichtzählbar	
Singular	Plural	Grundform	zählbare Ergänzung
box	*boxes*	*bread*	*loaves of bread*

Zählbar: box – boxes; bus – buses; car – cars; child – children; family – families; house – houses; knife – knives; radio – radios; woman – women

Nichtzählbar, zählbare Ergänzung: bread – loaves of bread; chocolate – bars of chocolate; coffee – cups of coffee; evidence – pieces of evidence; glass – sheets of glass; glue – tubes of glue; meat – slices of meat; oil – cans of oil; wine – bottles of wine

„Paarwörter"/Genitiv/Stützwort *„one/ones"*

„Paarwörter"

„Paarwörter" bezeichnen Dinge wie *scissors* (Schere) und *jeans* (Jeans), die aus zwei gleichen und miteinander verbundenen Teilen bestehen. Solche Nomen können wir **nur im Plural** gebrauchen. Wollen wir ein „Paarwort" **im Singular** oder **mit einem Zahlwort** im Plural benutzen, müssen wir *a/one pair of* ... bzw. *two/three/... pairs of* ... **hinzufügen.**

*Where **are** the **scissors?***

*I have only **one pair of jeans.***

Andere wichtige „Paarwörter" sind:

briefs	Slip
glasses	Brille
headphones	Kopfhörer
leggings	Leggings
(under)pants	Unterhose
pyjamas	Schlafanzug
shorts	kurze Hose, Shorts
swimming trunks	Badehose
tights	Strumpfhose
trousers	Hose

Der Genitiv

Bei **Personen** und bei **Tieren mit Namen** benutzen wir den *s*-Genitiv:

***My father's job** is not very interesting.*

*Where is **the dog's/Bruno's lead** (Leine)?*

Steht das Nomen im Singular oder endet der Plural nicht auf *-s*, hängen wir einfach 's an:

*The **men's toilet** is on the left.*

*This shop has **men's, women's** and **children's clothes.***

Endet der Plural auf *-s*, hängen wir nur ein Apostroph (') an:

*The **girls' team** won, but the **boys' team** lost.*

WISSEN • WISSEN • WISSEN • WISSEN • WISSEN • WISSEN • WISSEN

Bei **Sachen** benutzen wir den *of*-Genitiv:
*The man opened **the door of the car** without looking. A cyclist fell off his bike into **the middle of the road.***

Besonderheiten
Wenn das dazugehörige **Nomen schon vorher genannt** wurde, steht der *s*-Genitiv meist allein:
*Who does **this car** belong to?*
*It is **Nick King's.***

Bei **Ortsangaben** wie schon bekannten Wohnungen *(houses, flats)*, Geschäften *(shops, businesses)*, Restaurants usw. lassen wir das nachfolgende Nomen grundsätzlich weg:
*Please buy the sausages **at the butcher's,** okay?*
*I'll be late tomorrow. I'm going **to the dentist's.***

Bei **Zeitangaben** – *an hour's wait, this year's calendar, last night's TV programme* usw. – benutzen wir ebenfalls den *s*-Genitiv:
*Have you seen **today's paper** anywhere?*

■ **Das Stützwort *one/ones***
Wollen wir ein **zählbares Nomen** nicht wiederholen, können wir es durch *one* (Singular) bzw. *ones* (Plural) ersetzen.
*Do you want **the green T-shirt** or the **red one?***

*Did you see **the films** on BBC 1 last night?*
*No. I watched **the ones** on ITV.*

Anders als im Deutschen kann ein **Adjektiv** im Englischen **nicht allein** stehen.

4

Überprüfe hier, ob das Wissen sitzt

1 Setze passende „Paarwörter“ aus dem Kästchen in die richtigen Sätze ein.

glasses headphones jeans pliers *(Zange)* scarves scissors shoes shorts socks swimming trunks tights trainers

a I can't read what's on the blackboard without ________________.

b I wear ________________ in winter because they are warmer.

c Can't you use ____________________ to listen to that music? I'm on the phone.

d The trousers we call "_________" were first made by Levi Strauss in the USA.

e A lot of men prefer to wear ___________ rather than trousers in the summer.

f Do you have a pair of _________, please? I want to cut some wire.

2 Benutze die richtige Form des Genitivs.

a What is the *name of the capital of China* (name + capital + China) now, Bejing or Peking?

b There was an accident at the ______________________ (end + our street) today. The ________________ (front + a car) was badly damaged when it ran into the _______________ (back + a truck).

c Columbus died without knowing that his ________________________ (discovery + America) would change the ______________________ (history + the world).

d Joshua took ________________ (somebody + car) without permission.

e There was a time when there were no ____________________ (workers + rights). They were not even aloud to demonstrate outside the ________________________ (gates + factories).

f Have you seen ________________ (Fido + lead)? I though I left it on the ______________________ (top + the cupboard).

3 Vervollständige die Sätze mit *one/ones.*

a I tried to buy a map but the kiosk didn't have ______ .

b Josh didn't play as well in this match as he did in the last ______ .

c You can easily find our road. It's the ______ with a big filling station on the corner.

d We watched two films on TV last night but I didn't enjoy the second ______ much.

e Don't buy Spanish tomatoes. Please get Dutch ______ .

f These jeans cost € 125! Don't they have any cheaper ______ ?

g We didn't watch the documentary on Channel 1. We watched the ______ on Channel 4.

1 a glasses
b tights
c headphones
d jeans
e shorts
f pliers

2 b end of our street, front of a car, back of a truck
c discovery of America, history of the world
d somebody's car
e workers' rights, gates of factories
f Fido's lead, top of the cupboard

3 a one
b one
c one
d one
e ones
f ones
g one

Der bestimmte Artikel

Die **Schreibweise** des bestimmten Artikels bleibt immer unverändert: *the*. Die **Aussprache** dagegen ändert sich. Vor Konsonanten wird das *e* in *the* wie das *e* in „habe" ausgesprochen, vor Vokalen wie das *ie* in „Liebe".
The car** stopped outside **the shop.
*We live in **the old house** at **the end** of the road.*

Generell wird der bestimmte Artikel im Englischen viel weniger als im Deutschen benutzt. Aus diesem Grund haben die meisten Fehler mit dem unnötigen Gebrauch des Artikels zu tun.

Hat ein Nomen eine allgemeine, uneingeschränkte Bedeutung, dann steht es ohne Artikel.
***Violence** is increasing.*

Ist das Nomen näher beschrieben – also „bestimmt" –, dann benutzen wir *the*.
***The violence on TV** is particularly bad.*

Insbesondere wird der bestimmte Artikel in den folgenden Fällen und Wendungen im Englischen **nicht** gebraucht:

- **bei Namen von Straßen, Plätzen usw.:**
  *The cinema is **in Station Road.***
  Das Kino ist in der Bahnhofstraße.

  *Tourists like to sit **in Trafalgar Square.***
  Touristen sitzen gerne am (an dem) Trafalgar Square.

  ***Lake Constance** is Europe's biggest lake.*
  Der Bodensee ist Europas größter See.

- **bei Verkehrsmitteln:**
  *We go shopping **by bus.***
  Wir fahren mit dem Bus zum Einkaufen.

  *It is almost quicker to go **by train** than **by plane.***
  Es ist fast schneller mit dem Zug als mit dem Flugzeug.

- **bei Gebäuden und Ortsangaben im allgemeinen Sinn:**
  Mr Coe is ***in hospital.***
  Mr Coe liegt im (in dem) Krankenhaus.

  Do you go ***to school*** *on Saturdays?*
  Gehst du samstags in die Schule?

  The circus is ***in town*** *at the moment.*
  Zur Zeit ist der Zirkus in der Stadt.

- **bei Mahlzeiten als Zeitangaben:**
  I'm going shopping immediately ***after breakfast.***
  Ich gehe sofort nach dem Frühstück einkaufen.

  The power cut happened just ***before lunch.***
  Der Stromausfall trat direkt vor dem Mittagessen ein.

- **bei *most* in der Bedeutung von „die meisten“:**
  Most people *are friendly.*
  Die meisten Menschen sind freundlich.

Überprüfe hier, ob das Wissen sitzt

1 Benutze den bestimmten Artikel *the* nur, wenn notwendig. Sonst setze ein Kreuz (x) in die Lücke ein.

_______ accident took place in _______ Station Road near _______ hospital at about four o'clock in _______ afternoon. At first, _______ cause of _______ accident seemed clear. A woman in a blue Golf wanted to turn left on to _______ main road towards _______ town centre. Unfortunately, she did not see a motorcycle that was travelling in _______ same direction. _______ biker was unable to stop in _______ time and crashed into _______ Golf.

When _______ police arrived, _______ woman said, "I just can't understand it. Of course I saw _______ motorcycle, but I thought I had plenty of _______ space and _______ time." "Well, you were wrong, madam," said _______ police officer. "I'm afraid _______ people often misjudge *(falsch einschätzen)* both _______ speed and _______ distance."

At that moment, a man spoke. "Excuse me," he said, but I saw what happened and _______ lady is quite right. _________ fact is that _________ motorcycle suddenly accelerated *(beschleunigen)* so that she didn't have _______ time to get out on to _________ main road. That was _______ real cause of _______ accident, officer."

2 Vervollständige die Übersetzungen.

a Am besten fährt man nach Paris mit dem Zug.

It's best to travel ____________________________________.

b Am Wochenende gibt es eine Kirmes in der Stadt.

There is a fair ____________________________________.

c Der nächste Supermarkt ist in der London Road.

The nearest supermarket ____________________________________.

d Ist Düsseldorf auch am Rhein?

Is Düsseldorf also ____________________________________?

e Die meisten Hunde sind harmlos.

____________________________________ harmless.

f Momentan ist sein Vater im Gefängnis.

His father is ____________________________________.

1 *The* accident took place in *x* Station Road near *the* hospital at about four o'clock in *the* afternoon. At first, *the* cause of *the* accident seemed clear. A woman in a blue Golf wanted to turn left on to *the* main road towards *the* town centre. Unfortunately, she did not see a motorcycle that was travelling in *the* same direction. *The* biker was unable to stop in *x* time and crashed into *the* Golf.

When *the* police arrived, *the* woman said, „I just can't understand it. Of course I saw *the* motorcycle, but I thought I had plenty of *x* space and *x* time." „Well, you were wrong, madam," said *the* police officer. „I'm afraid *x* people often misjudge both *x* speed and *x* distance."

At that moment, a man spoke. „Excuse me," he said, but I saw what happened and *the* lady is quite right. *The* fact is that *the* motorcycle suddenly accelerated so that she didn't have *x* time to get out on to *the* main road. That was *the* real cause of *the* accident, officer."

2
a to Paris by train
b in town at the weekend
c is in London Road
d on the Rhine
e Most dogs are
f in prison at the moment

Der unbestimmte Artikel

Beginnt das Wort unmittelbar nach dem Artikel mit einem **Konsonanten,** benutzen wir *a*. Wenn das Wort mit einem **ausgesprochenen Vokal** beginnt, benutzen wir *an*.

Can I have ***a banana*** *and* ***a big glass*** *of milk, please?*

Don't eat ***an ice****. Have* ***an apple*** *or* ***an orange.***

Entscheidend dabei ist, wie der Anfangslaut des Wortes ausgesprochen – nicht geschrieben – wird.

Do all British schools have ***a uniform?***

Our bus goes in ***an hour.***

Anders als im Deutschen benutzen wir im Englischen den unbestimmten Artikel in den folgenden Fällen:

- **bei Berufsangaben:**
  Helen is ***a teacher*** *and John* ***an engineer.***
  Helen ist Lehrerin und John Ingenieur.

- **bei Angaben über Nationalität, Religion, Politik:**
  Is Birgit ***an Austrian*** *or* ***a German?***
  Ist Birgit Österreicherin oder Deutsche?

  Was Lincoln ***a Democrat*** *or* ***a Republican?***
  War Lincoln Demokrat oder Republikaner?

- **bei den meisten Bagatellkrankheiten:**
  Sally has got ***a cold.***
  Sally ist erkältet.

  I've got ***an awful headache.***
  Ich habe schreckliche Kopfschmerzen.

- **bei nachgestellten Maß- und Zeitangaben:**
  How much are these apples ***a kilo?***
  Wie viel kosten diese Äpfel pro Kilo?

  Petrol costs £ 1.10 ***a litre.***
  Benzin kostet 1.10 £ pro Liter.

You may only drive at 30 kilometres ***an hour*** *here.*
Hier darfst du nur 30 Kilometer in der Stunde fahren.

We have English three times ***a week.***
Wir haben Englisch dreimal in der Woche.

- **bei den folgenden Wendungen:**

to be in a hurry	in Eile sein, es eilig haben
to come to an end	enden
for a change	zur Abwechslung
for a long time	lange Zeit
for a short time	kurze Zeit
to have a bath	sich baden
to have a go	es versuchen
to have a shave	sich rasieren
to have a shower	sich duschen
to have a wash	sich waschen
in a loud voice	mit lauter Stimme
to make a noise	Lärm machen
to take a seat	Platz nehmen
What a pity!	Wie schade!
without a break	ohne Pause

Beachte: Bei *half, quite, rather, such* wird *a/an* nachgestellt.
Hurry up. We've only got ***half an hour.***
Beeil dich! Wir haben nur eine halbe Stunde.

We had ***quite a good holiday*** *in Holland.*
Wir hatten einen ganz guten Urlaub in Holland.

Tom can be ***rather a silly boy.***
Tom kann ein ziemlich alberner Junge sein.

I've never read ***such an interesting book.***
Ich habe noch nie so ein interessantes Buch gelesen.

■ Überprüfe hier, ob das Wissen sitzt

1 Setze *a* bzw. *an* ein.

a _______ apple
b _______ cabbage
c _______ egg
d _______ hamburger
e _______ lemon
f _______ orange
g _______ bottle of ketchup
h _______ can of peas
i _______ expensive piece of meat
j _______ ice cream
k _______ old roll
l _______ pound of butter

2 Setze die Wörter bzw. Ausdrücke aus den Klammern in die Sätze ein. Benutze den unbestimmten Artikel *a/an,* wenn notwendig.

a I've seldom seen ______________________________ as *Casablanca*.
(such, good film)

b We didn't even get a menu for ______________________________ .
(half, hour)

c Joshua can be ________________________ when he loses his temper.
(rather, idiot)

d ___________________________________ to say! (What, rude thing)

e My brother had ______________________________ on holiday.
(quite, nice time)

f ___________________________________ you sometimes see on TV.
(What, nonsense)

3 Vervollständige die Übersetzung ins Englische.

a Sei vorsichtig! Heute ist der Chef schlechter Laune.

Be careful! The boss ______________________________ today.

b Ist es wahr, dass einige Ärzte zehn Stunden ohne Pause arbeiten?

Is it true that some doctors work ______________________________

______________________________ ?

c Birgt duscht sich gerade.

Birgit ______________________________ at the moment.

d Es ist schade, aber alle guten Dinge gehen zu Ende.

______________________________ , but all good things come

______________________________ .

1
a *an* apple
b *a* cabbage
c *an* egg
d *a* hamburger
e *a* lemon
f *an* orange
g *a* bottle of ketchup
h *a* can of peas
i *an* expensive piece of meat
j *an* ice cream
k *an* old roll
l *a* pound of butter

2
a such a good film
b half an hour
c rather an idiot
d What a rude thing
e quite a nice time
f What nonsense

3
a is in a bad mood
b for ten hours with a break
c is having a shower
d It's a pity, to an end

Some, any und ihre Zusammensetzungen

Möchten wir über eine **unbestimmte Menge** *(indefinite quantity)* reden, benutzen wir *some* oder *any* („einige", „etwas"). Die beiden Wörter haben die gleiche Bedeutung, werden aber unterschiedlich eingesetzt.
Wir benutzen *some* in **bejahten Aussagen** und *any* in **verneinten Aussagen** und Fragen.
Please don't forget to buy ***some apples.***
We haven't got ***any coffee.***
Have we got ***any wine,*** *Helen?*

Ist eine Frage eigentlich eine höfliche **Bitte,** benutzen wir *some*. Dasselbe gilt auch für **Angebote.**
Have you got ***some salt,*** *please?*
Would you like ***some salad,*** *Tom?*

Wir benutzen die **Zusammensetzungen** von *some* und *any* – *somebody/anybody, someone/anyone, something/anything, somewhere/anywhere* – in genau derselben Art und Weise.
Listen! I think there is ***somebody*** *at the door.*
Really? I didn't hear ***anything.***
I can't find my cap ***anywhere.*** *I expect I left it* ***somewhere*** *in town.*

Im Englischen benutzen wir *some* und *any* auch, wenn wir im Deutschen „etwas" oder „einige" weglassen würden:
Helen must buy ***some wine.***
Helen muss Wein kaufen.

Wir benutzen *any* im Sinne von *it doesn't matter which* (es spielt keine Rolle, welche) auch in Aussagen:
You can come ***any day*** *after 5 o'clock.*
I'd like ***any Madonna CD,*** *please.*

Beachte, dass *some* mit dieser Bedeutung nicht benutzt werden kann!

Überprüfe hier, ob das Wissen sitzt

1 Setze *some* oder *any* in die Sätze ein.

a Do you have _________ mustard, please?

b We don't need _________ bread.

c There is _________ butter in the kitchen.

d It was awful. _________ men had too much to drink and started a fight.

e Would you like _________ more fries? You can have _________ of mine. I don't want _________ more.

f The party was a bit boring because there wasn't _________ music.

g Don't forget to buy _________ milk or we won't have _________ for breakfast.

2 Vervollständige die Sätze mit *somebody/anybody, something/anything* oder *somewhere/anywhere.*

a I can't find my red sweatshirt. Have you seen it _____________?

b I need _____________ to help me fix my bike. Can you think of _____________ I could ask?

c Do you know _____________ about how mobile phones work?

d We're advertising for _____________ to work in our IT department. Do you know _____________ with the necessary qualifications?

1
a any
b any
c some
d Some
e some – some – any
f any
g some – any

2
a anywhere
b somebody – anybody
c anything
d somebody – anybody

8

Many, much, a lot of, plenty of und *few*

Wir benutzen *many* mit zählbaren Nomen und *much* mit nichtzählbaren Nomen in **verneinten Aussagen** oder **Fragen.**
*We don't have **many rolls.***
*How **many tomatoes** have we got?*
*People don't eat **much beef** nowadays.*
*Why did you buy so **much cheese?***

In **bejahten Aussagen** benutzen wir *a lot of* mit zählbaren sowie nichtzählbaren Nomen.
*We have **a lot of apples** and **a lot of bread**, too.*

Sehr häufig können wir *much* bzw. *many* durch *a lot of* ersetzen, nicht aber nach *as, so, too, how* und *very.*
*Don't eat **so much cake.** There's **too much sugar** in it.*

Möchten wir „mehr als genug" ausdrücken, können wir *a lot of* durch *plenty of* ersetzen.
*We have **plenty of rolls.** And **plenty of butter** as well.*

■ *A little/little, a few/few*

Wir benutzen *a little* (= ein wenig) und *little* (= wenig) mit nichtzählbaren und *a few* (= ein paar) und *few* (= wenige) mit zählbaren Nomen. Dies gilt für **alle Satzarten,** also für bejahte und verneinte Aussagen und Fragen.
*Would you like **a little water** with your whiskey?*
*Can I have **a few potatoes,** please?*
*I'm afraid some pupils show **little interest** in school.*
***Few players** are as good as he is.*

Überprüfe hier, ob das Wissen sitzt

1 Vervollständige die Sätze mit *a little/little* oder *a few/few*.

a Can I give you ______________ more fries?

No, thanks, but I'd like ______________ bread, please.

b Nobody gets fat at Brenda's parties. You only get ______________ muesli.

Not quite. Last time we got ______________ bits of cheese, too.

c Most doctors say that you should use only ______________ salt.

Sure, but only ______________ doctors follow their own advice.

2 Übersetze die Ausdrücke ins Englische. Benutze *much/many/a lot of/ plenty of* bzw. *(a) few/(a) little*.

a mehr als genug Brötchen ______________________________

b wenig Interesse ______________________________

c viel Ärger ______________________________

d wenig Wasser ______________________________

e ein paar Hunde ______________________________

f ein wenig verärgert ______________________________

g viele Lehrer ______________________________

h wenige Freunde ______________________________

i viel Glück/Spaß ______________________________

1 a a few – a little
b a little – a few
c a little – a few

2 a plenty of rolls
b little interest
c a lot of/much trouble
d little water
e a few dogs
f a little annoyed
g a lot of/many teachers
h few friends
i a lot of/much luck/fun

9

Each und every

Every bedeutet „alle ohne Ausnahme" und *each* etwa „jeder Einzelne aus einer begrenzten Anzahl".
Da von der Bedeutung her *each* und *every* sehr ähnlich sind, können wir die beiden Wörter **beliebig** einsetzen – vorausgesetzt, dass sie **unmittelbar vor einem Nomen** stehen.
We go cycling ***each/every weekend.***
The police questioned ***each/every person*** *in the room.*

Trotz dieser Bedeutungsähnlichkeit gibt es Fälle, in denen **nur** *each* infrage kommt:

- E*ach* ist die einzige Möglichkeit bei einer Auswahl von zwei.
  The two teams both scored a goal in ***each half.***

- *Every* kann nur vor einem Nomen benutzt werden. Deshalb ist *each* die einzige Möglichkeit vor einer *of*-Fügung und wenn das Wort allein – also ohne Nomen – steht.
  Each of the girls *won a prize.*
  These four bikes cost over €2,000 ***each.***

WISSEN • WISSEN • WISSEN • WISSEN • WISSEN • WISSEN • WISSEN

Überprüfe hier, ob das Wissen sitzt

Verbinde einen Satzteil aus der linken Liste mit einem passenden aus der Liste rechts, um sinnvolle Sätze mit *each/every* zu bilden, z. B.:
The pizzas I bought cost € 10 each.

a The pizzas I bought	at every meeting this year.
b The teacher wants to speak	cost € 10 each.
c The police stopped each of	did very well in the test.
d We have two cakes and	each one tastes wonderful.
e Every family I know is	worried about money at present.
f Mr Gregg gave each of his	grandchildren a book.
g We spend every New Year's Eve	on the North Sea coast.
h Ted and Ben go to the	to each boy alone.
i Each of the pupils in the class	the drivers for speeding.
j We have discussed this problem	pub every day.

b The teacher wants to speak to each boy alone.
c The police stopped each of the drivers for speeding.
d We have two cakes and each one tastes wonderful.
e Every family I know is worried about money at the moment.
f Mr Gregg gave each of his grandchildren a book.
g We spend every New Year's Eve on the North Sea coast.
h Ted and Ben go to the pub every day.
i Each of the pupils in the class did very well in the test.
j We have discussed this problem at every meeting this year.

10

Die Personalpronomen

Personalpronomen können Nomen ersetzen. Wir benutzen sie unter anderem, um eine eintönige Wiederholung von Namen und Nomen zu vermeiden. Im Englischen – ganz anders als im Deutschen – benutzen wir immer *it* für **Sachen** und **Tiere.** Die „geschlechtsanzeigenden" Pronomen *he* und *she* werden nur für **Menschen** und Haustiere verwendet. Personalpronomen können sowohl **Subjekt** als auch **Objekt** eines Satzes sein.

■ Subjektform

Tom is British. ***He*** *lives in London.*
Helen is Scottish. ***She*** *lives in Stirling.*
Alan and Lucy are Welsh. ***They*** *live near Conway.*

■ Objektform

Where's Helen? I haven't seen ***her*** *today.*
Please visit ***us*** *when you're in Bristol.*
That man hit ***me*** *with his umbrella.*
Can you lend ***me*** *your bike, please? I'll bring* ***it*** *back tomorrow.*

Die Personalpronomen

Subjekt		**Objekt** (wem?, wen? oder was?)
I	ich	*me*
you	du/Sie	*you*
he	er	*him*
she	sie	*her*
it	es/er/sie	*it*
we	wir	*us*
you	ihr/Sie	*you*
they	sie	*them*

Überprüfe hier, ob das Wissen sitzt

Setze die richtigen Personalpronomen ein.

a David — Where are ______ from, Halina?

Halina — ______ am from Gdansk. ______ is in Poland.

David — ______ know. In German ______ is Danzig.

Halina — And what about ______ , David? Where do ______ live?

David — ______ live in Bristol.

Halina — Oh, yes. That's like Alice. ______ lives in Bristol, too.

David — Yes. ______ are siblings *(Geschwister)*.

b Pierre — Hi, Anna. ______ would like to introduce Inga and Vadim. ______ are two new students.

Anna — Hi. ____ is nice to meet ______. Where are ______ from?

Inga — ______ are from St Petersburg. That's in Russia.

Anna — _____ know. _____ is a beautiful city. My dad went there and _____ says _____ is most beautiful city _____ has ever visited.

a Where are *you* from, Halina?
I am from Gdansk. *It* is in Poland.
I know. In German *it* is Danzig.
And what about *you*, David? Where do *you* live?
I live in Bristol.
Oh, yes. That's like Alice. *She* lives in Bristol, too.
Yes. *We* are siblings.

b Hi, Anna. *I* would like to introduce Inga and Vadim. *They* are two new students.
Hi. *It* is nice to meet *you*. Where are *you* from?
We are from St Petersburg. That's in Russia.
I know. *It* is a beautiful city. My dad went there and *he* says *it* is most beautiful city *he* has ever visited.

Die Possessivadjektive

Die **Possessivadjektive** sagen uns, wem irgendetwas gehört. Sie stehen immer **unmittelbar vor dem entsprechenden Nomen,** genau wie ein Adjektiv.
Beachte die **Schreibweise** von *its*. Diese wird manchmal mit *it's* (Kurzform von *it is*) verwechselt.
Beachte die **Schreibweise** von *their* (ihr/ihre). Diese wird häufig mit *there* (da/dort) verwechselt.
Im Englischen verwenden wir Possessivadjektive bei **Körperteilen** und **Kleidungsstücken.** Im Deutschen hingegen benutzen wir meist den bestimmten Artikel (die Hände, den Mantel).
Sally hasn't finished ***her homework*** *yet.*
Is that ***their new car?***
Please wash ***your hands*** *before eating.*
Helen left ***her coat*** *on the bus.*
Look at that bird. It has hurt ***its wing.***

Die Possessivadjektive

I	***my***
you	***your***
he	***his***
she	***her***
it	***its***

we	***our***
you	***your***
they	***their***

Überprüfe hier, ob das Wissen sitzt

Übersetze den markierten Teil der Sätze ins Englische. Benutze Possessivadjektive.

a Wie ist Ihr Name, bitte?

____

b Ist der Golf sein Auto?

____

c Anna schreibt ihrer Familie eine Ansichtskarte.

____

d Die Studenten müssen ihre Bücher selbst kaufen.

____

e Wir dürfen unsere Laptops nicht benutzen.

____

f Der Polizist fragte mich nach meiner Adresse.

____

g Dieses Zimmer ist viel zu klein für unsere Gruppe.

____

h Die Studenten sagen, dass ihr Lehrer nicht erschienen sei.

____

i Sie dürfen Ihr Auto hier nicht parken.

____

a your name
b his car
c her family
d their books
e our laptops
f my address
g our group
h their teacher
i your car

Die Possessivpronomen

Mine und *hers* sind Possessivpronomen, die allein – also **ohne Nomen** – stehen.
Possessivpronomen werden statt eines schon erwähnten Possessivadjektivs + Nomen *(your coat)* benutzt. Wir vermeiden dadurch lästige Wiederholungen.

Is this your coat, Helen?
No, it's not ***mine.*** *Ask Sally.*
You're right. It must be ***hers.***

Die Possessivpronomen

I	***mine***
you	***yours***
he	***his***
she	***hers***
it	–
we	***ours***
you	***yours***
they	***theirs***

Überprüfe hier, ob das Wissen sitzt

Ersetze die markierten Ausdrücke durch Possessivpronomen.

a That bike is my bike (________). Why don't you use your bike (________)?

Because my bike (________) is broken, that's why I need your bike (____________).

b Sara's cooking is much better than Janna's. Janna's cooking (________) is awful. It's nearly as bad as my cooking (__________)!

c That mobile isn't my mobile (________). I think it's Ben's.

No, it's not Ben's (________). He has a Sony.

d Jane and Sara's flat is bigger than Ben's and my flat (________).

Their flat (________) has three bedrooms, but our flat (________) has only two, you see.

Well, your flat (________) is bigger than Joshua and Ann's flat.

I think their flat (________) has only one bedroom.

a That bike is *mine*. Why don't you use *yours*?
Because *mine* is broken, that's why I need *yours*.

b Sara's cooking is much better than Janna's. *Hers* is awful. It's nearly as bad as *mine*!

c That mobile isn't *mine*. I think it's Ben's.
No, it's not *his*. He has a Sony.

d Jane and Sara's flat is bigger than *ours*. *Theirs* has three bedrooms, but *ours* has only two, you see.
Well, *yours* is bigger than Joshua and Ann's flat. I think *theirs* has only one bedroom.

13

Self-pronouns (reflexive pronouns)

Self-Pronomen – oder Reflexivpronomen – beziehen sich auf das **Subjekt** des Satzes. Wir benutzen sie also, wenn das Objekt dieselbe Person oder Sache wie das Subjekt ist.
*Jane **hurt herself** when she fell off her bike.*
*Mr and Mrs Coe are both over 80 but they still **look after themselves.***

Wir benutzen *self*-Pronomen auch, wenn wir betonen möchten, dass eine **bestimmte Person** irgendetwas selbst tut oder getan hat. Bei diesem Gebrauch benutzen wir im Deutschen „selbst" oder „selber".
*We never buy vegetables. **My dad grows** them **himself.***

Die *self*-Pronomen

I	***myself***
you	***yourself***
he	***himself***
she	***herself***
it	***itself***
we	***ourselves***
you	***yourselves***
they	***themselves***

Beachte die Schreibweise der Pluralformen: *ourselves, yourselves, ...*

Self-Pronomen werden im Englischen viel seltener als im Deutschen verwendet. Beachte, dass die folgenden deutschen Verben im Englischen **kein *self*-Pronomen** haben:

sich ändern	*to change*
sich beeilen	*to hurry up*
sich beklagen	*to complain*
sich bewegen	*to move*
sich erinnern	*to remember*
sich entschuldigen	*to apologise*
sich entspannen	*to relax*
sich fragen	*to wonder*
sich freuen auf	*to look forward to*
sich fühlen	*to feel*
sich fürchten	*to be afraid*
sich hinlegen	*to lie down*
sich hinsetzen	*to sit down*
sich öffnen	*to open*
sich Sorgen machen	*to worry*
sich streiten	*to quarrel*
sich treffen	*to meet*
sich verändern	*to change*
sich verstecken	*to hide*
sich (etwas) vorstellen	*to imagine (something)*
aber:	
sich amüsieren	*to enjoy oneself*

■ *Each other/one another*

Die beiden Pronomen *each other/one another* haben dieselbe Bedeutung und die gleiche Form für alle Personen. Es ist also einerlei, welches der beiden Pronomen benutzt wird. Möchten wir eine **wechselseitige Beziehung** ausdrücken, benutzen wir *each other/one another* statt eines *self*-Pronomens.

*We always help **each other** with our homework.*
*Mr and Mrs Green often argue with **one another.***

Überprüfe hier, ob das Wissen sitzt

1 Setze die richtige Form des *self*-Pronomens in die Lücken ein.

a The cow hurt __________ when it fell over.

b I ____________ would prefer to stay at home this weekend.

c The Greens never cook ____________________ . They always eat out.

d Kevin, you'll have to leave the room if you can't behave ___________ .

e Mrs Cobb didn't introduce _____________ to the class at all.

f We need help. We can't do this job _________________ .

g Look, kids, if you can't do your homework ____________ , I'll help you.

h Tom promised me ______________ that he wouldn't be late.

2 Setze ein *self*-Pronomen oder ein Objektpronomen *(me, you, him, her, ...)* je nach Sinn des Satzes in die Lücken ein.

a In a test, always ask _______________ this question: "What does the examiner *(Prüfer)* expect _________ to tell __________ ?".

b We haven't time to show _____________ round now. I'm afraid you'll just have to look after ___________________ until we get home.

c Dennis is only interested in ______________ . But what about __________ and our children? He never thinks of __________ .

d A lot of people buy material from a do-it-_______________ store and then carry out repairs ____________________ . This may save __________ some money, but what about professional builders? It's really hard on __________ .

e Don't talk to ________ about ________ , Joe. Talk to Ann about it _______________ .

f This problem isn't going to solve __________, is it? We have to sort

________ out _________________.

3 Vervollständige die Sätze mit einem *self*-Pronomen oder *each other* (drückt Gegenseitigkeit aus).

a People who get married should love __________________ not

____________________.

b Couples who can't imagine living with __________________ for ever shouldn't marry.

c Just look at __________________, Frank! What on earth have you been up to?

d The idea of having a business partner is that you help ____________.

e Psychologists say that most of us talk to __________________ more than to __________________.

1 a itself
b myself
c themselves
d yourself
e herself
f ourselves
g yourselves
h himself

2 a yourself – me – him
b you – yourselves
c himself – me – us
d yourself – themselves – them – them
e me – it – yourself
f itself – it – ourselves

3 a each other – themselves
b each other
c yourself
d each other
e ourselves – each other

14

Die Demonstrativpronomen

This (Singular) und *these* (Plural) verwenden wir bei sich **in der Nähe** befindenden Personen und Dingen. Sie entsprechen also den deutschen Pronomen „diese/dieser/dieses ...".

This book *(here) belongs to Helen.*

Can I borrow ***these CDs*** *(here), please?*

That (Singular) und *those* (Plural) benutzen wir bei **weiter entfernten** Personen und Dingen. Sie entsprechen den deutschen Pronomen „jene/jener/jenes ...".

Is ***that man*** *(over there) your English teacher?*

Do ***those boys*** *(over there) go to your school, too?*

Demonstrativpronomen können auch **zeitlich** benutzt werden. In dieser Anwendung bedeuten *these* etwa „jetzt" und *that/those* „in der (meist entfernteren) Vergangenheit":

Life has become more complicated ***these days.***

Heutzutage ist das Leben viel komplizierter geworden.

At that time *I was working in New York.*

Zu jener Zeit/Damals arbeitete ich in New York.

In those days *most people worked on the land.*

In jenen Tagen/Damals arbeiteten die meisten Menschen auf dem Lande.

Überprüfe hier, ob das Wissen sitzt

Setze das richtige Demonstrativpronomen in die Sätze ein.

a The traffic warden *(Politesse)* stood beside the car. "_________ car can't stay here," she said.

b The teacher pointed to the broken chairs. "How did _________ two chairs get broken?" he asked.

c The boy threw a stone at a bird. A man spoke to him. "_________ was a horrible thing to do," he said.

d The teacher picked up the books. "Who do _________ books belong to?" she asked.

e The Snows met ten years ago. In _________ days they were both working in Berlin.

f Put out _________ cigarette, will you? You aren't allowed to smoke in pubs _________ days.

g "Look at _________ photo in the paper. Isn't _________ the man we saw in town yesterday?"

h Ben looked across the room. "_________ woman over there looks just like Julia Roberts," he said.

i You can't talk about historical events without understanding what life was like in _________ times.

j "I find _________ texts here rather difficult. I can't understand _________ word, for example."

a This
b those
c That
d these
e those
f that – these
g this – this
h That
i those
j these – this

15

Die Adjektive (Gebrauch)

Wir benutzen Adjektive, um **Personen** und **Sachen** näher zu beschreiben. Genau wie im Deutschen stehen Adjektive entweder unmittelbar **vor einem Nomen** oder **nach einer Form von *be* oder *become*.**

*Tom has bought a **new** car.*

*German **is difficult** to learn.*

Es gibt auch eine kleine Zahl von **Verben der sinnlichen Wahrnehmung** *(sense verbs)*, die ebenfalls von Adjektiven – nicht also Adverbien – beschrieben werden.

Die wichtigsten sind: *to feel* (sich fühlen), *to look* (aussehen), *to seem* (scheinen), *to smell* (duften, riechen), *to sound* (klingen), *to taste* (schmecken).

*Helen **looks beautiful** today.*

*This cake **tastes good!***

Überprüfe hier, ob das Wissen sitzt

Lies den Text und unterstreiche alle Adjektive.

a Jake and Janna's new neighbour, Mr Parks, was polite and friendly but he also seemed a real eccentric *(Ekzentriker)*. He always wore a long, black coat and an old hat, even on warm summer days. And he always carried a yellow umbrella with him, even on dry, sunny days when the weather was good.

b And Mr Parks looked funny as well. With his round head, little ears and big, thick glasses he looked like an owl. But they say that owls are wise *(klug)* birds and Mr Parks was similar to owls there, too, because he was very clever.

c One day, Jake and Janna had some difficult Biology homework. "This is terrible," said Janna in a hopeless voice. "I can't even understand the stupid questions so how can I answer them?" "Look," said Jake. "Let's ask Mr Parks if he can help us. I know he's very interested in nature." "Cool," said Janna. "Let's go."

d When Mr Parks looked at the questions, he said, "of course I'll help you. Actually, you are lucky. This is my special area of interest."

a new, polite, friendly, real, long, black, old, warm, yellow, dry, sunny, good
b funny, round, little, big, thick, wise, similar, clever
c difficult, terrible, hopeless, stupid, interested, cool
d lucky, special

Die Steigerung von Adjektiven

Im Englischen kennen wir die ***-er/-est*-Steigerung** und die ***more/most*-Steigerung.**

*Tom is **fast**, isn't he? Yes, but Ben is **faster.***
*You're right. He's **the fastest runner.***

*Is Paris **bigger** than London?*
*Helen is **the happiest girl** I know. She's **the nicest,** too.*

*This bike is **more expensive** than that one.*
*Sure, but the red one is the **most expensive bike** of all.*

Wir benutzen die ***-er/-est*-Steigerung** für alle **einsilbigen Adjektive:**

	-er	*-est*
big	*bigger*	*biggest*
clean	*cleaner*	*cleanest*
fast	*faster*	*fastest*

Beachte die Schreibweise: Der Endkonsonant nach einem kurzen Vokal wird verdoppelt und das stumme (= nicht ausgesprochene) *-e* fällt weg.

Und für alle **zweisilbigen Adjektive, die auf *-y* enden:**

	-er	*-est*
early	*earlier*	*earliest*
happy	*happier*	*happiest*
lucky	*luckier*	*luckiest*
silly	*sillier*	*silliest*

Beim Anhängen von *-er/-est* wird das *-y* zum *-i.*

Wir benutzen die ***more/most*-Steigerung** für **zweisilbige Adjektive, die nicht auf *-y* enden:**

	more	*most*
boring	*more boring*	*most boring*
careful	*more careful*	*most careful*
famous	*more famous*	*most famous*
helpful	*more helpful*	*most helpful*

und für alle **mehrsilbigen Adjektive:**

beautiful	*more beautiful*	*most beautiful*
difficult	*more difficult*	*most difficult*
expensive	*more expensive*	*most expensive*
interesting	*more interesting*	*most interesting*

Bei einer kleinen Zahl von zweisilbigen Adjektiven sind beide Steigerungen – also *-er/-est* oder *more/most* – möglich:
*Jane is **cleverer/more clever** than Jill.*

Die wichtigsten Adjektive dieser Gruppe sind:
cruel (grausam), *pleasant* (angenehm), *polite* (höflich), *quiet* (ruhig, still), *stupid* (dumm), *tired* (müde)

sowie alle Adjektive, die auf *-er, -le, -ow* enden, z. B.:
clever (klug), *gentle* (sanft), *simple* (einfach)

Überprüfe hier, ob das Wissen sitzt

1 Vervollständige die Tabelle. Trage die englische Übersetzung der Adjektive und ihre englischen Steigerungsformen ein.

	deutsch	Grundform	Komparativ	Superlativ
a	billig			
b	gefährlich			
c	groß	big		
d	dumm			
e	hübsch			
f	interessant			
g	nett			
h	ruhig			
i	schnell			
j	schön			
k	schwierig			

2 Benutze die richtige Form der Adjektive, um sinnvolle Sätze zu bilden.

a Ben isn't very ________________ (satisfied) with life at the moment because he has a rather __________ (boring) job. Still, I'm _______ (sure) he will be ____________ (happy) when they give him some ___________________________ (interesting) work.

b Everybody knows that ____________ (happy) people work _______ (good). Our boss should be ______________________ (appreciative – *anerkennend*) and he could be a lot _____________ (friendly), too.

c Do you think it is _______ (true) that Italians, say, are ____________ (friendly) and ________________________ (tolerant) than Germans, for example?

No, I don't. It depends completely on the person. In fact, one of the _______________ (friendly) people I know happens to be a German and one of the ______________________ (intolerant) is an Italian!

1
a cheap, cheaper, cheapest
b dangerous, more dangerous, most dangerous
c big, bigger, biggest
d stupid, more stupid, most stupid (*auch* stupider, stupidest)
e pretty, prettier, prettiest
f interesting, more interesting, most interesting
g nice, nicer, nicest
h quiet, more quiet, most quiet (*auch* quieter, quietest)
i fast, faster, fastest
j beautiful, more beautiful, most beautiful
k difficult, more difficult, most difficult

2
a satisfied – boring – sure – happier – more interesting
b happier – better – more appreciative – more friendly/friendlier
c true – more friendly/friendlier – more tolerant – friendliest – most intolerant

Unregelmäßige Steigerungen und Vergleiche in Sätzen

Diese Adjektive werden **unregelmäßig** gesteigert:
*It is **better** to eat apples than sweets.*

Grundform	Komparativ	Superlativ	deutsch
bad	*worse*	*worst*	schlecht
far	*further*	*furthest*	weit
good	*better*	*best*	gut
a lot of, lots of	*more*	*most*	viel(e)
many	*more*	*most*	viele
much	*more*	*most*	viel
some	*more*	*most*	einige
a few, few	*less*	*least*	wenig(e)
a little, little	*less*	*least*	wenig(e)

Beachte: *little* in der Bedeutung von „klein" kann nicht gesteigert werden. Deshalb benutzen wir *small – smaller – smallest*.

Vergleiche in Sätzen

Möchten wir **Personen** oder **Sachen** im Satz miteinander vergleichen, haben wir die folgenden Möglichkeiten:

as ... as	genauso ... wie	*Is Munich **as big as** Hamburg?*
not as ... as	nicht so ... wie	*Amsterdam is **not as big as** Berlin.*
more/less ... than	mehr/weniger ... als	*I find books **more interesting than** television.* *English is **less difficult than** German.*

Überprüfe hier, ob das Wissen sitzt

1 Ergänze die fehlenden Formen.

			schlecht
			weit
			viel
			einige
			wenig(e)

2 Stelle Vergleiche in Sätzen her. Verwende die Adjektive aus den Klammern.

a Hamburg has about 1.7 million inhabitants *(Bewohner)*, and Munich has around 1.4. (small)

____

b Ben's flat is 65 square metres and so is ours. (big)

____

c There are three kids in my family. I'm fifteen, my brother Tony is ten and my sister Madison is twelve. (young)

____

____

1

bad	worse	worst	schlecht
far	further	furthest	weit
much	more	most	viel
some	more	most	einige
a few, few	less	least	wenig(e)

2
a Munich is smaller than Hamburg.
b Our flat is as big as Ben's.
c Tony is two years younger than Madison. He is the youngest child in the family.

TESTEN • TESTEN • TESTEN • TESTEN • TESTEN • TESTEN • TESTEN • TESTEN

18

Adjektive und Adverbien im Vergleich

Der Gebrauch von Adjektiven

Möchten wir Personen oder Sachen näher beschreiben, benutzen wir Adjektive:

*Ben Scott is a **fascinating** man.*
*I think Paris is **more exciting** than Berlin.*

Adjektive stehen **unmittelbar vor Nomen** oder **nach einer Form von *be* bzw. *become*** (werden) **oder *seem*** (scheinen), die *be* ersetzen können:

*Helen works for a **big firm** in London. Her job **is interesting** and she **seems happy** there.*

Wir verwenden Adjektive auch mit **Verben** wie *to feel* (sich fühlen), *to look* (aussehen), *to sound* (klingen), *to smell* (duften, riechen) und *to taste* (schmecken), die eine sinnliche Wahrnehmung ausdrücken:

*Bob **looks sad** today.*
*A lot of pupils **feel bored** at school.*

Der Gebrauch von Adverbien

Möchten wir ein **Tätigkeitsverb** näher beschreiben, muss ein Adverb folgen:

*Always **drive slowly** near schools.*
*Harry always **works carefully** and **neatly.***
*Please **speak loudly.** Mrs Coe can't **hear well.***

Wir benutzen Adverbien auch, um **Adjektive, andere Adverbien** und **ganze Sätze** näher zu bestimmen:

*Our team is **surprisingly good** at the moment.*
*The meal was **absolutely terrible.***
*I'm afraid some boys behaved **very badly.***
*Tom sang **surprisingly well.***
***Unfortunately** we missed our bus.*
***Luckily** the doctor was at home.*

Überprüfe hier, ob das Wissen sitzt

Benutze die Adverbform der Adjektive, wenn notwendig (siehe auch Seite 56/57).

Italian lemon chicken

a Wash and dry chicken. Cut chicken into eight pieces. Heat (large) ________ pan and fry chicken pieces until brown.

b Chop *(klein schneiden)* one onion, two tomatoes and four carrots. When chicken pieces are (ready) ________, put to one side for later.

c Fry onion in butter and then add tomatoes, chopped carrot and a piece of lemon peel *(Schale)*. Mix (careful) ______________.

d Season *(würzen)* mixture (generous) ________________ with rosemary; add salt and pepper.

e Put chicken pieces in mixture and cook (slow) __________ for about an hour.

f Stir mixture (occasion) ____________________.

How to prepare the lemon sauce:

g Put two spoonfuls of flour into a big glass. Add a little milk and mix until smooth *(klumpenfrei)*. Add rest of milk (gradual) __________; stir (constant) __________________. Beat two eggs and the juice of a large lemon in a bowl.

h When the chicken is cooked, add milk and flour and stir (good) ________. Take pan from heat and add eggs. Mix and return pan to heat until sauce becomes (thick) ________.

a	large	e	slowly
b	ready	f	occasionally
c	carefully	g	gradually – constantly
d	generously	h	well – thick

19

Die *ly*-Adverbien

Wir bilden die weitaus meisten Adverbien durch das einfache **Anhängen von -*ly*** an das entsprechende Adjektiv.
*Please come **quickly**.*
*You should go to the dentist **regularly**.*

Beim Anhängen von -*ly* gibt es einige wichtige **Schreibregeln.**

Endet das Adjektiv auf -*y*, wird das -*y* zu -*i*:
*The driver shouted **angrily** at the cyclist.*

angry	→	*angrily*
easy	→	*easily*
happy	→	*happily*
hungry	→	*hungrily*
thirsty	→	*thirstily*
aber:		
shy	→	*shyly* (schüchtern)

Endet das Adjektiv auf -*le*, fällt das -*e* weg:
*The play was **terribly** funny.*

probable	→	*probably*
simple	→	*simply*
terrible	→	*terribly*

Endet das Adjektiv auf *-ic*, wird *-ally* angehängt:
*Manchester United is playing **fantastically** well.*

automatic	→	*automatically*
basic	→	*basically*
enthusiastic	→	*enthusiastically*
fantastic	→	*fantastically*
systematic	→	*systematically*

Einige Adjektive – am wichtigsten *friendly, lively, lovely, silly* und *ugly* – enden schon auf *-ly*. Um das Adverb zu bilden, benutzen wir das unveränderte Adjektiv mit der **Umschreibung** *in (such) a ... way:*
*Sarah alway treats people **in a friendly way.***
*Why are you speaking **in such a silly way?***
*The man looked at the child **in an ugly way.***

Überprüfe hier, ob das Wissen sitzt

1 Bilde die Adverbform der englischen Adjektive und schreibe die deutsche Bedeutung dazu. Achte auf die Rechtschreibung.

Adjektiv	Adverb	deutsch
angry		
automatic		
busy		
enthusiastic		
happy		
hungry		
possible		
thirsty		
shy		
simple		
careful		
noisy		
polite		

2 Setze die englische Entsprechung der deutschen Adverbien (in Klammern) in die Sätze ein. Benutze den Ausdruck *in a … way,* wo notwendig.

a Games are no fun if people don't play ________________ *(fair).*

b Please talk ________________ in the church *(leise).*

c Sean often behaves ________________ in lessons *(albern).*

d Nowadays you can ________________ find information on the internet *(leicht).*

e It's a fact that bullies *(fig. Tyrannen)* often behave ________ *(feige).*

f Julie didn't check her test ________________ enough *(gründlich).*

g You must drive past schools ________________ *(langsam).*

h Don't eat so ________________ *(gierig).* People are looking at you.

1

Adjektiv	Adverb	deutsch
angry	angrily	verärgert
automatic	automatically	automatisch
busy	busily	eifrig
enthusiastic	enthusiastically	begeistert
happy	happily	glücklich
hungry	hungrily	hungrig
possible	possibly	möglich
thirsty	thirstily	durstig
shy	shyly	schüchtern
simple	simply	einfach
careful	carefully	vorsichtig
noisy	noisily	laut
polite	politely	höflich

2
a fairly
b quietly
c in a silly way
d easily
e in a cowardly way
f thoroughly
g slowly
h greedily

20

Unregelmäßige Adverbien

Die Adverbien *early, fast, long* und *straight* (sofort) haben **dieselbe Form wie** das entsprechende **Adjektiv.**
*Jane always comes **early.***
*Don't speak so **fast.** I can't understand you.*

Einige Adverbien haben **zwei Formen,** eine wie das Adjektiv und eine auf *-ly.* Die beiden Formen haben **unterschiedliche Bedeutungen.**
*Why do you always come **late?***
*Have you seen Jim **lately?***
*No. I **hardly** ever see him nowadays.*

Die wichtigsten Adverbien dieser Gruppe sind:

Adverbform = Adjektivform		*-ly*-Adverb	
close	nah	*closely*	sorgfältig
deep	tief	*deeply*	zutiefst
fair	gerecht	*fairly*	ziemlich
hard	hart	*hardly*	kaum
high	hoch	*highly*	höchst
late	spät	*lately*	neulich
most	meist	*mostly*	meistens
near	nah	*nearly*	fast
pretty	ziemlich	*prettily*	hübsch
short	kurz	*shortly*	bald
wide	breit	*widely*	überall

Die Adverbform von *good* ist *well.*
*I'm pleased. You're playing **well** at the moment.*

Überprüfe hier, ob das Wissen sitzt

Vervollständige die englischen Übersetzungen.

a Zwei Menschen wurden in dem Unfall ziemlich ernsthaft verletzt.

Two people were ______________________________

in the accident.

b Der Redner sollte lauter sprechen. Wir können ihn kaum hören.

The speaker should speak ______________________ . We

can ______________________ .

c Viele Eltern sind der Meinung, dass fast alle Klassen zu groß sind.

A lot of parents are of the opinion that ______________________

______________________________ .

d Dieser Käse ist viel zu hart und er ist auch zu alt.

This cheese is ______________________ and

______________________ .

e Der Zug kam zu spät an. Dies ist neulich oft passiert.

The train arrived ______________________ . This has

happened ______________________ .

f Nach der Vorstellung fuhren wir direkt nach Hause.

After the performance we ______________________ .

g Die zwei Flugzeuge sind fast kollidiert.

The two aircraft ______________________ .

a pretty seriously injured
b louder, hardly hear him
c nearly all classes are too big
d much too hard, it is also too old
e late, often lately
f drove straight home
g nearly collided

21

Die Steigerung von Adverbien und Vergleiche

Endet das Adverb auf *-ly*, steigern wir mit *more/most*.
*I wish people would work **more carefully.***
*Jane works **most carefully** in our office.*

Hat das Adverb **dieselbe Form** wie das Adjektiv, steigern wir mit *-er/-est*.
*You must work **harder** or you'll lose your job.*
*Helen left the office **earliest.***

Diese Steigerungen sind **unregelmäßig:**

well	*better*	*best*
badly	*worse*	*worst*

Vergleiche in Sätzen

Möchten wir **Personen** oder **Dinge im Satz** miteinander vergleichen, haben wir die folgenden Möglichkeiten:

as ... as	genauso ... wie	*Does Tom work **as well as** the others?*
not as ... as	nicht so ... wie	*My car does **not** go **as fast as** Mike's.*
more/less ... than	mehr/weniger ... als	*Sally works **more systematically than** Brenda.* *Helen speaks German **less fluently than** Ben.*

Deutschsprachige Schülerinnen und Schüler machen leicht Fehler, indem sie *so* statt *as* verwenden oder indem sie *as* einsetzen, wo *than* richtig wäre.
*This T-shirt is not ~~so~~ **as** cheap as that one.*
*My dog is cleverer ~~as~~ **than** yours.*

Überprüfe hier, ob das Wissen sitzt

Suche für jeden Satz ein passendes Adverb aus dem Kasten aus und setze es in der richtigen Form ein.

badly cheaply dangerously early fast gently
hard long politely quickly violently well

a I find violent action films silly. People behave much ______________ ____________ in them than in real life.

b Julie did really well in the Maths test. She did even ______________ than last time.

c It was awful. Our team played ___________ of all the teams in the competition.

d Don't be so rude. If you can't speak ______________________, then don't speak at all.

e Ben was there first. He arrived _______________ than anybody else.

f Janna won the race. She ran ____________________________________.

g You can buy DVDs _____________________________ at discount stores than at other shops.

h Don't be rough. You should treat babies ____________________ than that.

a more violently
b better
c worst
d more politely
e earlier
f fastest
g more cheaply
h more gently

TESTEN • TESTEN • TESTEN • TESTEN • TESTEN • TESTEN • TESTEN • TESTEN

22

Arten von Adverbien und ihre Stellung

Satzadverbien

Satzadverbien – wie *fortunately/unfortunately* (leider), *in fact* (in der Tat), *luckily* (glücklicherweise)/*unluckily, maybe* (vielleicht), *naturally* (natürlich), *obviously* (offensichtlich), *of course* (selbstverständlich) und *perhaps* (vielleicht) – bestimmen einen ganzen Satz.
Daher stehen sie am **Satzanfang.**
Luckily *the rain soon stopped.*
Maybe *we can find a taxi.*
Of course *you can borrow my bike.*

Adverbien der Art und Weise

Adverbien der Art und Weise (Hilfsfrage: Wie?) – z. B. *badly, beautifully, politely* (höflich), *quickly, shortly* (barsch) usw. – stehen in der Regel am **Satzende.**
The car was going too ***quickly.***
The man spoke to us ***politely.***

Zeit- und Ortsadverbien

Zeitadverbien (Hilfsfrage: Wann?) und Ortsadverbien (Hilfsfragen: Wo?, Wohin?) stehen in der Regel am **Satzende.**
Helen went home ***at 3 o'clock.***
Tom lives ***in London.***

Stehen ein Zeitadverb und ein Ortsadverb zusammen am Satzende, dann gilt die **Reihenfolge Ort vor Zeit** (O vor Z):
Our plane leaves ***New York at 10.30.***

Eine Anreihung von Orts- bzw. Zeitadverbien am Satzende wird **vom Spezifischen zum Allgemeinen** geordnet:
Our plane lands ***at 10.30 on 10 May.***
They live ***in a flat in Church Lane in York.***

Kommt ein Adverb der Art und Weise dazu, ist die **Reihenfolge Art und Weise – Ort – Zeit** (*Manner – Place – Time*):
Mary sang ***beautifully at the concert last night.***

Häufigkeitsadverbien

Besteht ein Häufigkeitsadverb aus einem Wort – z. B. *always, never, often, sometimes* –, steht es unmittelbar **vor dem Vollverb** bzw. **nach einer Form von *be*.**

*Helen **always** walks to the office.*
*Tom is **sometimes** late for work.*

Besteht das Adverb aus mehr als einem Wort – z. B. *every day, now and then* –, steht es wie ein Zeitadverb **am Satzende.**

*We go shopping **every Saturday.***

Gradadverbien

Gradadverbien – z. B. *a bit* (ein bisschen), *absolutely, completely* (völlig), *hardly* (kaum), *nearly* (fast), *pretty* (ziemlich), *rather* (ziemlich), *really* (eigentlich, wirklich), *totally, very, wholly* (gänzlich) – haben die gleiche Position wie Adjektive. Sie stehen unmittelbar **vor dem Wort, das sie beschreiben.**

*The baby **nearly** died.*
*Are you **completely** certain?*
*The film was **quite** good.*
*Harry behaved **a bit** stupidly at the party.*

Überprüfe hier, ob das Wissen sitzt

1 Welche Position im Satz gilt für die angegebenen Adverbien? Kreuze die richtige Spalte an.

Adverb	Satzanfang	Satzmitte	Satzende
now and then			
of course			
in Berlin			
at 7 o'clock			
every day			
often			
completely			
sometimes			
beautifully			
unfortunately			
rather			
at home			

2 Stelle die Adverbien an die richtige Position im Satz wie im Beispiel a.

a Harry goes + to school/every morning/at 8 o'clock

Harry goes to school at 8 o'clock every morning.

b My father was born + 1985/on 6 April/at midnight

____

c Betty has breakfast + before going to work/never

____

d Our Biology teacher shouted at us + in class/very rudely/today

____

e I missed my bus + this morning, unfortunately

____

f Janna is unhappy + rather, at the moment, of course

____

g Ben understands German but he can't speak it + very fluently/quite well

____

h I'll meet you + tomorrow afternoon/outside the town hall/at 4 o'clock

____

1

Adverb	Satzanfang	Satzmitte	Satzende
now and then			x
of course	x		
in Berlin			x
at 7 o'clock			x
every day			x
often		x	
completely		x	
sometimes		x	
beautifully			x
unfortunately	x		
rather		x	
at home			x

2
b My father was born at midnight on 6 April 1985.
c Betty never has breakfast before going to work.
d Our Biology teacher shouted at us very rudely in class today.
e Unfortunately I missed my bus this morning.
f Of course Janna is rather unhappy at the moment.
g Ben understands German quite well but he can't speak it very fluently.
h I'll meet you outside the town hall at 4 o'clock tomorrow afternoon.

23

Die Konjunktionen

Wir benutzen **Konjunktionen,** um Wörter, Satzglieder oder Sätze miteinander zu verbinden.
Helen likes fruit ***and*** *vegetables.*
You can walk ***or*** *go by bus.*
Tom tried on the trousers, ***but*** *they were too big.*
Dad was in the garden ***when*** *I saw him.*
I was late ***because*** *my bus didn't come.*
We lost the game ***although/though*** *we had trained hard.*

Die häufigsten Konjunktionen sind:

although	obwohl
and	und
as soon as	sobald
because	weil
because of	wegen
but	aber
however	jedoch
or	oder
though	obwohl
when	als, wenn

Die Konjunktion *when* hat zwei Bedeutungen:
It started to rain ***when*** *we were waiting for the bus.*
Es fing an zu regen, **als** wir auf den Bus warteten.

Can you give Kate this book ***when*** *you see her?*
Kannst du Kate dieses Buch geben, **wenn** du sie siehst?

Überprüfe hier, ob das Wissen sitzt

Streiche die falsche bzw. wenig geeignete Konjunktion durch.

a They took the injured dog to the vet ~~and~~/but he was dead ~~as~~/when they got there.

b It was snowing hard when/and they arrived in Scotland.

c I'm afraid Brenda will never be able to play chess well although/however she tries very hard.

d Harry is a brilliant billiards-player and/or he travels to competitions all over Europe.

e I sometimes go to a fortune-teller but/or I don't really believe what I am told.

f Of course you can go to the party as long as/when you're back home by midnight.

g We saw Jenny Coe go by in her car so/while we were waiting at the bus stop.

h I don't think we'll win the match although/no matter how we train for it.

i Do you think we need to reserve a table at the restaurant if/when we go as soon as they open?

j Tom was not only late for the lesson and/but he was very rude to the teacher as well.

k Sarah can't come to the party because/for she is not feeling very well.

Die passenden Konjunktionen sind:

b when
c although
d and
e but
f as long as
g while
h no matter how
i if
j but
k because

Das Verb *be*

Wir können das Verb *be* alleine als **Vollverb** benutzen und als ein **Hilfsverb,** um die *progressive*-Zeiten oder das Passiv zu bilden.

*Berlin **is** the German capital now but it **was** Bonn.*

- ***Is** Tom there, please?*
- *No, he **isn't (is not)** here. He**'s (is)** on holiday this week.*

*Helen **is cooking** at the moment.*

*Our car **was made** in France.*

In **verneinten Sätzen** benutzen wir *be* genau wie „sein" im Deutschen. Normalerweise verwenden wir in der gesprochenen Sprache und in privaten Briefen die **Kurzform,** wie in den folgenden Tabellen angegeben.

***Present* (Präsens)**

bejaht		verneint	
*I **am***	*I'm*	*I am not*	*I'm not*
*you **are***	*you're*	*you are not*	*you're not, you aren't*
*he **is***	*he's*	*he is not*	*he's not, he isn't*
*she **is***	*she's*	*she is not*	*she's not, she isn't*
*it **is***	*it's*	*it is not*	*it's not, it isn't*
*we **are***	*we're*	*we are not*	*we're not, we aren't*
*you **are***	*you're*	*you are not*	*you're not, you aren't*
*they **are***	*they're*	*they are not*	*they're not, they aren't*

Bei der **Verneinung** gibt es – mit Ausnahme der 1. Person Singular – **zwei Kurzformen.** Entweder können wir das Pronomen *(I, you, he, ...)* mit dem Verbteil kombinieren oder den Verbteil mit *not*:

***She's not** from Vienna.*

***They're not** from Vienna.*

***They aren't** from Vienna.*

Past (Präteritum/Imperfekt)

bejaht	verneint	
*I **was***	*I was not*	*I wasn't*
*you **were***	*you were not*	*you weren't*
*he **was***	*he was not*	*he wasn't*
*she **was***	*she was not*	*she wasn't*
*it **was***	*it was not*	*it wasn't*
*we **were***	*we were not*	*we weren't*
*you **were***	*you were not*	*you weren't*
*they **were***	*they were not*	*they weren't*

Die Partizipien

Die Partizipien von *be* lauten:

being	*-ing*-Form	(Partizip Präsens)
been	3. Form	(Partizip Perfekt)

There + eine Form von *be*

Mit *there* + einer Form von *be* drücken wir aus, dass irgendetwas vorhanden ist, passiert ist oder existiert.

Im Deutschen wird diese Idee meist durch eine Form von „es gibt ..." ausgedrückt.

***There is** some milk in the fridge.*

Es gibt etwas Milch im Kühlschrank.

***There was** a bad accident in town yesterday.*

Es gab gestern einen schlimmen Unfall in der Stadt.

*Do you think **there is** life on Mars?*

Glauben Sie, dass es Leben auf dem Mars gibt?

Überprüfe hier, ob das Wissen sitzt

1 Benutze die richtige Form der Gegenwart von *be*.

a They ____________ our new neighbours.

b I ____________ your new English teacher.

c Ben ____________ Julie's boyfriend.

d That mobile phone ____________ Sally's.

e My best friend and I ____________ American.

2 Benutze die richtige Form der Vergangenheit von *be*.

a We ________ late because our bus ____________ late.

b I ____________ very tired last night.

c Barbara ____________ at the cinema, too.

d The Greens ____________ in Croatia last Easter.

e You ____________ rude to say that, Josh.

3 Formuliere die Sätze in verneinte Aussagen und Fragen um. Bei der Verneinung benutze die lange und die kurze Form.

a Barbara is very clever.

____________________________ very clever.

____________________________ very clever?

b We were late for Julie's party.

____________________________ late for Julie's party.

____________________________ for Julie's party?

c I was rude to the Biology teacher.

I ____________________________ rude to the Biology teacher.

____________________________ was rude to the Biology teacher?

d It is my turn to clean the blackboard.

__________________________ my turn to clean the blackboard.

__________________________ my turn to clean the blackboard?

e You are interested in handball, aren't you?

__________________________ interested in handball, are you?

__________________________ interested in handball?

4 Vervollständige die Übersetzungen.

a Es hat keinen Zweck, darüber zu streiten.

__________________________ in arguing about it.

b Es waren viele Leute im Freibad heute.

__________________________ in the open-air pool today.

c Gibt es eine Tankstelle in der Nähe?

__________________________ around here?

d Gibt es noch Fragen, bitte?

__________________________, please?

1 a are
b am
c is
d is
e are

2 a were, was
b was
c was
d were
e were

3 a Barbara is not/isn't
Is Barbara
b We were not/weren't
Were we

c was not/wasn't
Was I
d It is not/isn't
Is it
e You are not/aren't
Are you

4 a There is no point
b There were a lot of people
c Is here a filling station
d Are there any more questions

25

Das Verb *have*

Als **Vollverb** bedeutet *have* „haben", „besitzen".
In der Gegenwart *(present)* benutzen wir – vor allem im britischen Englisch – *have got*.
Dies bedeutet, dass bei **Fragen** und der **Verneinung** eine Umschreibung mit *do/does* entfällt.
*Helen **has got** a car.*
***Has Helen got** a car?*
*Tom and Helen **haven't got** any children yet.*

Benutzen wir *have* ohne *got,* dann bilden wir **Fragen** und die **Verneinung** mit *do/does.*
*Helen **has** a car.*
***Does** Helen **have** a car?*
*Tom and Helen **don't have** any children yet.*

In der **Vergangenheit** wird *got* meist nicht benutzt. Daher bilden wir Fragen und die Verneinung mit *did:*
***Did you have** a nice meal last night?*
*No, **we didn't have** a nice one at all. It was awful.*

In der **gesprochenen Sprache** benutzen wir meist nur die **Kurzform.**
Als **Hilfsverb** benutzen wir *have,* um die *perfect*-Zeiten zu bilden:
*I **have worked** here since last July.*

Present (Präsens)

bejaht		verneint	
lang	kurz	lang	kurz
*I **have***	*I've*	*I have not*	*I haven't*
*you **have***	*you've*	*you have not*	*you haven't*
*he **has***	*he's*	*he has not*	*he hasn't*
*she **has***	*she's*	*she has not*	*she hasn't*
*it **has***	*it's*	*it has not*	*it hasn't*
*we **have***	*we've*	*we have not*	*we haven't*
*you **have***	*you've*	*you have not*	*you haven't*
*they **have***	*they've*	*they have not*	*they haven't*

Die **Kurzformen** von *he/she/it **is*** und von *he/she/it **has*** sind identisch: *he's, she's, it's*. Ob es sich um *is* oder *has* handelt, ist jedoch leicht aus dem jeweiligen Zusammenhang zu erkennen.

Past (Präteritum/Imperfekt)

Das *past* von *have* heißt ***had.*** Die verneinte Form ist *had not* (Langform) bzw. *hadn't* (Kurzform). Dies gilt bei allen Personen.

Die Partizipien

having	*-ing*-Form	(Partizip Präsens)
had	3. Form	(Partizip Perfekt)

Überprüfe hier, ob das Wissen sitzt

1 Setze die richtige Form des Präsens von *have* in die Sätze ein. Bei Fragen und Verneinungen, benutze beide Formen, also *do/does, got,* und die Kurzform. Schau dir das Beispiel an.
Do you have/Have you got any cheaper T-shirts?
I don't have/haven't got much money with me.

a I ______________________________ a job. I'm still at school.

b Our class ___________ 35 people in it but our classroom only ____________ 15 desks.

c Nowadays, most computers __________ three or four USB sockets.

d We ________________________ that DVD, but we can order it.

e The students all ____________________ their books with them.

f Peter _____________ a car, but he _____________ a scooter.

g ____________________________________ a weekend job?
No. I _____________________ enough time because of football.

h This radio is useless. It ______________________ any batteries.

i Frank ________________________ the talent to play the guitar.

2 Benutze die Vergangenheit von *have*.

a We __________ a lot of snow yesterday.

b I wanted to see the film but unfortunately I _____________ the time.

c ____________________________ a chance to speak to her? Yes, I did.

d The Greens ______________ a terrible argument in the supermarket.

e Julie ___________________ enough money with her to buy any wine.

f You ______________________________ a valid ticket to get in, I hope.

1
a don't have – haven't got
b has, has
c have
d don't have – haven't got
e have
f doesn't have – hasn't got, has
g Do you have – Have you got, don't have – haven't got
h doesn't have – hasn't got
i doesn't have – hasn't got

2
a had
b didn't have
c Did you have
d had
e didn't have
f had

Das Verb *do*

Als **Vollverb** bedeutet *do* „erledigen“ bzw. „machen“. Verwenden wir *do* als Vollverb, bilden wir die **Verneinung** und **Fragen** ebenfalls mit *do.*
Dann erscheint *do* natürlich zweimal im Satz, erst als Hilfsverb und dann als Vollverb im Infinitiv.
*Tom usually **does** the shopping.*
*I **did** my homework on Sunday.*
*I **don't do** my homework as soon as I get home.*
***Do** you **do** the cooking, too, Tom?*

Bei allen Vollverben benutzen wir *do* als **Hilfsverb,** um die **Verneinung, Fragen** und die **verneinte Befehlsform** zu bilden.
*We **didn't go** on holiday last summer.*
***Do** Helen and Tom **work** for the same firm?*
***Don't shout.** Put up your hand.*

Genau wie bei *be* und *have* benutzen wir in der gesprochenen Sprache und in Privatbriefen meist die **Kurzform:**
*You **don't** know Sally Wood, do you?*
*Tom **doesn't** like curry.*
*I **didn't** enjoy the film much.*

Present (Präsens)

bejaht	verneint	
lang	lang	kurz
I ***do***	*I do not*	*I don't*
you ***do***	*you do not*	*you don't*
he ***does***	*he does not*	*he doesn't*
she ***does***	*she does not*	*she doesn't*
it ***does***	*it does not*	*it doesn't*
we ***do***	*we do not*	*we don't*
you ***do***	*you do not*	*you don't*
they ***do***	*they do not*	*they don't*

Past (Präteritum/Imperfekt)

Das *past* von *do* heißt ***did.*** Die verneinte Form ist ***did not*** (Langform) bzw. *didn't* (Kurzform). Dies gilt bei allen Personen.

Die Partizipien

doing	*-ing*-Form	(Partizip Präsens)
done	3. Form	(Partizip Perfekt)

■ Überprüfe hier, ob das Wissen sitzt

1 Vervollständige die Ausdrücke mit *do* oder *make*.

a (to) ________________ a noise

b (to) ________________ one's homework

c (to) ________________ the washing-up

d (to) ________________ fun of sb.

e (to) ________________ one's best

f (to) ________________ business with sb.

g (to) ________________ certain/sure of sth.

h (to) ________________ without sth.

2 Setze *do/does* oder *did* in die Sätze ein.

a What ________________ you ________________ last weekend?

b How ________________ you ________________, Mr Carr? It's nice to meet you.

c In the past, most people ________________ without things like foreign holidays.

d When ________________ you usually ________________ your homework?

e We ________________ a lot of business with his firm last year.

f Why should I always ________________ the washing-up? I ________________ it yesterday.

3 Benutze die Elemente, um Sätze mit einer Form von *do* zu bilden. Füge fehlende Wörter hinzu.

a Susan/not like/film/much/last night/.

Susan ____

____

b you + play/football/every Saturday/?

____

____ every Saturday?

c How often/Harry + help/house/? ____________________________

____house?

d Jenna and Joshua/normally/do/shopping/weekend/.

Jenna and Joshua normally ____________________________

____

1
a make
b do
c do
d make
e do
f do
g make
h do

2
a What *did* you *do* last weekend?
b How *do* you *do*, Mr Carr? It's nice to meet you.
c In the past, most people *did* without things like foreign holidays.
d When *do* you usually *do* your homework?
e We *did* a lot of business with his firm last year.
f Why should I always *do* the washing-up? I *did* it yesterday.

3
a Susan didn't like the film much last night.
b Do you play football every Saturday?
c How often does Harry help in the house?
d Jenna and Joshua normally do the shopping at the weekend.

Das *simple present*

Mit **Ausnahme der 3. Person Singular** hat bei Vollverben das *simple present* immer dieselbe Form wie der Infinitiv. Bei *he/she/it* wird ein *-s* angehängt.
*Tom **lives** in Southport but he **works** in Liverpool.*
*I **take** the train to Liverpool every morning.*
*In the evening the Greens usually **watch** television.*

Es gibt folgende Schreibregeln beim Anhängen von *-s:*
Bei einem Zischlaut *(-ch, -sh, -ss, -x)* benutzen wir *-es:*

teach	→	*teaches*
wash	→	*washes*
miss	→	*misses*
fix	→	*fixes*

Das *-y* nach einem Konsonanten wird zum *-i.* Hinzu kommt *-es:*

fly	→	*flies*
try	→	*tries*

Das *-y* nach einem Vokal bleibt dagegen unverändert:

buy	→	*buys*
stay	→	*stays*

Ist kein Hilfsverb im Satz vorhanden, bilden wir die **Verneinung** mit *do not (don't)/does not (doesn't).*

Beachte: Das Vollverb steht bei der Verneinung immer im **Infinitiv.**
*Tom **doesn't go** (does not go) to work by bus.*

Fragen

Für Fragen gilt Folgendes: Gibt es **kein Hilfsverb** im Satz, werden Fragen ebenfalls **mit *do/does*** gebildet.

*Tom, **do you go** to work by car or by train?*

Bei Fragen mit *what?* und *who?* verfahren wir anders. Ist *what?* bzw. *who?* das **Subjekt** des Satzes, dann benötigen wir kein Hilfsverb, um Fragen zu bilden:

***What happens** when you are late for school?*
***Who teaches** you English?*

Ist aber das Fragewort das **Objekt** des Satzes, dann bilden wir Fragen mit einem Hilfsverb, also wie gewöhnlich:

***What does** this word **mean** in English?*
***Who do you like** best, Tom or Ben?*

Wir benutzen das *simple present,* um zu sagen, was immer so ist oder was man immer wieder macht.

Die folgenden **Zeitangaben** kommen sehr häufig mit dem *simple present* vor:

always, never, often, seldom/rarely (selten), *sometimes, now and then* (ab und zu)
usually, normally, regularly, generally (im Allgemeinen), *as a rule* (in der Regel)
every day/week/month/..., on Mondays/..., at weekends/Christmas/...

Grundsätzlich benutzen wir das *simple present,* um über den **Inhalt von Texten** (hier J.B. Priestley's *An Inspector Calls*) zu sprechen:

*The policeman **visits** the Birlings and **tells** them about the girl's suicide. He **questions** each member of the family and **shows** that they **are** all partly responsible* (verantwortlich) *for her death.*

Überprüfe hier, ob das Wissen sitzt

1 Setze die Verben in das *simple present* ein. Achte auf verneinte Aussagen und Fragen.

a The Kings ________ (live) in Bristol. Sarah King ________(be) still at school, but her parents and brother, Ben, all _________ (have) jobs.

b Sarah's father _____________ (teach) at a school in St Paul's. Her mother ________________ (not work) full-time. Ben _______ (be) a motor mechanic. He ______________ (work) at a garage in Clifton.

c Ben and his American friend Hank often ________ (meet) on the internet. They ______________ (not know) each other personally, but they _______ (keep) in touch by email. They ________ (hope) to meet personally in the summer.

d The Kings ________ (have) a car but they ______________ (not use) it often because petrol _________ (cost) so much. Ben and his dad usually ________ (walk) to work, and Sarah ________ (go) to school by bike. Mrs King ___________ (not go) out to work. Her customers ________ (come) to her home where she _______ (cut) their hair.

e On his way to work, Nick always ________ (buy) a newspaper for his boss, Dave Budd. When Nick __________ (leave) the garage in the afternoon, Dave always ________ (say), "Nick, I _______ (hope) you _________________ (not forget) my paper tomorrow" and Nick always ______________ (answer), "_____________________ (I + ever forget) your paper, Dave? That ___________ (seem) to be my most important job."

2 Vervollständige die Übersetzungen der Fragen ins Englische.

a Meinen Sie, dass Sarah verärgert ist?

____ that Sarah is angry?

b Sind die Browns im Urlaub?

____ on holiday?

c Sieht Robert häufig fern?

____ TV?

d Geben wir zu viel Geld für Lebensmittel aus?

____ on food?

1
a live – is – have
b teaches – does not work – is – works
c meet – do not know – keep – hope
d have – do not use – costs – walk – goes – does not go – come – cuts
e buys – leaves – says – hope – don't forget – answers – Do I ever forget – seems
f don't meet – studies – wants – don't like – think – spends – worry

2
a Do you think
b Are the Browns
c Does Robert often watch
d Do we spend too much money

28

Das *present progressive*

Wir bilden das ***present progressive*** mit *am/is/are* + *-ing*-Form des Vollverbs.
*Tom **is washing** his car at the moment.*

Bei Verben, die auf *-e* enden, lassen wir bei der Bildung der *-ing*-Form den Endbuchstaben *-e* weg:

come → *coming*
make → *making*

Bei Verben, die auf *-ie* enden, wird das *-ie* zum *-y:*

die → *dying*
lie → *lying*

Bei Verben, die mit einem kurzen Vokal + folgendem Konsonanten wie *-m, -n, -p* oder *-t* enden, wird der Konsonant verdoppelt:

run → *running*
stop → *stopping*
put → *putting*

Da beim *present progressive* immer ein Hilfsverb *(am/is/are)* vorhanden ist, wird die **Verneinung** mit *not/n't* gebildet:
*I **am not/I'm not feeling** very well at present.*

Um **Fragen** zu bilden, tauschen wir *am/is/are* und das Subjekt einfach aus:
***Is Helen working** in London now?*

Wir benutzen das *present progressive,* um zu sagen, was **im Moment** des Sprechens oder Schreibens tatsächlich passiert. Im Deutschen gibt es keine vergleichbare Verbform; wir benutzen stattdessen Ausdrücke wie „gerade", „dabei sein, etwas zu tun".

Wir verwenden das *present progressive* auch für **vorübergehende Ausnahmen:**
*We normally go out on Friday evenings, but today we **are staying** at home.*

Das *present progressive* kommt häufig mit den **Zeitangaben** *at present* (zur Zeit), *at the moment* und *now* vor.

Achtung: Die folgenden Verben haben **keine** *progressive*-Form:
to be
to believe (glauben)
to dislike (nicht mögen)
to hate
to know
to like
to love
to mean (bedeuten)
to notice (bemerken)
to see
to seem (scheinen)
to want
to wish (wünschen).

Überprüfe hier, ob das Wissen sitzt

1 Vervollständige die Tabelle mit den fehlenden *-ing*-Formen. Achte auf die Schreibweise.

Infinitiv	*-ing*-Form
(to) bake	
(to) become	
(to) begin	
(to) control	
(to) die	
(to) get	
(to) joke	
(to) lie	
(to) live	
(to) take	
(to) tie	
(to) travel	

2 Vervollständige die Sätze mit dem *simple present* oder mit dem *present progressive.*

a Jane and Kate usually ____________________ (work) in the office but we ____________________ (be) so busy today that they ______________ ___________ (help) in the shop.

b I ____________________ (not go) to school by bus. I usually __________ ___________ (walk), but I ____________________ (catch) the bus today because it ____________________ (rain).

c I ________________ (be) afraid the firm ________________ (not do) well at present. In fact, we ________________ (lose) money.

d Barbara still ________________ (live) with her parents but she ________________ (look for) a flat of her own.

e Sue ________________ (not help) Mum. She ________________ (read) in her room.

f Brenda's horrible. We ________________ (not talk) to each other at present.

3 Übersetze die Sätze ins Englische.

a Sei ruhig. Kate spricht gerade am Telefon.

____

b Ich will nicht so viele Stunden arbeiten, aber wir brauchen das Geld.

____

c Normalerweise sehen wir fern, aber heute gehen wir ins Kino.

____

1 *-ing*-Form:
baking
becoming
beginning
controlling
dying
getting
joking
lying
living
taking
tying
travelling

2 a work – are – are helping
b don't go – walk – am catching – is raining
c am – is not doing – are losing
d lives – is looking for
e is not helping – is reading
f are not talking

3 a Be quiet. Kate is speaking on the phone.
b I don't want to work so many hours, but we need the money.
c Normally we watch TV but today we are going to the cinema.

29

Das *present perfect*

Wir bilden das **present perfect** mit dem Hilfsverb *have/has* + Partizip Perfekt (3. Form).
*Tom **has bought** a new bike. It's American.*
*Mr and Mrs Coe **have lived** here for over 50 years.*

Bei **regelmäßigen Verben** hat das Partizip dieselbe Form wie die des *simple past,* also Infinitiv + *-ed.*
*Helen **has** just **arrived**.*

Die **unregelmäßigen Verben** dagegen haben eine besondere Form, die man sich einfach merken muss.
*The bus still **has not/hasn't come** yet. It's late again.*
***Have** you **seen** the film at the ABC yet?*
*I **have done** my homework. I can come now.*

Die **Verneinung** wird durch das Einfügen von *not/n't* unmittelbar nach dem Hilfsverb *have/has* gebildet.

Um **Fragen** zu bilden, tauschen wir *have/has* und das Subjekt einfach aus.

Wenn wir sagen, dass etwas in der **Vergangenheit** geschehen ist, **ohne den Zeitpunkt des Geschehens zu nennen,** benutzen wir das *present perfect*.

Oft benutzen wir das *present perfect* für **Handlungen** bzw. **Situationen,** die in der Vergangenheit angefangen haben, aber noch andauern. Sie sind also **noch nicht abgeschlossen.**

Bei diesem Gebrauch tritt das *present perfect* oft mit den folgenden **Zeitangaben** auf:

before	(hier:) bisher
for	seit (Dauer, z.B. *for two hours*)
since	seit (Zeitpunkt, z.B. *since 7 o'clock*)
already	schon
yet	schon
not yet	bis jetzt noch nicht
ever	jemals
never	bisher noch nie
so far	bisher
still not	immer noch nicht
till/until now	bis jetzt
up to now	bis jetzt

Achtung Fehlerquelle: In solchen Fällen benutzen wir im Deutschen das Präsens:

*I **have lived** here for three years.*
Ich wohne hier seit drei Jahren.

Wir benutzen das *present perfect* auch, wenn wir über die **Auswirkung einer Handlung** sprechen wollen. Nur das **gegenwärtige Ergebnis** interessiert uns.
Dieser Gebrauch wird häufig durch die Zeitangabe *just* (soeben, gerade) signalisiert.
Das *present perfect* kommt häufig in **Fragen** mit *yet* und *ever* (schon einmal) sowie in **negativen Aussagen** mit *not ... yet* (noch nicht) und *never* vor:

***Has Tom ever been** to the USA?*
War Tom jemals in den USA?

They haven't done** their homework **yet.
Sie haben ihre Hausaufgaben noch nicht gemacht.

*I **have never heard** such a silly idea.*
Ich habe noch nie so eine dumme Idee gehört.

Überprüfe hier, ob das Wissen sitzt

1 Bilde die richtige Form des *present perfect*. Achte auf verneinte Aussagen und Fragen.

a ______________________________ (the film/start) yet?

b Carol and Jack ____________________ (not leave) for school yet.

c Our team ______________ (win) their third match since October.

d I ______________________________ (just + switch on) my computer.

e Sally, ______________________ (you/finish) your homework?

f They ________________ (not visit) their grandparents for years.

g We ______________________ (not have) a holiday since 2001.

h ___________________________ (you/see) Josh anywhere?

i Why ______________________________ (Janna/go) home?

She ________________________ (not write) those letters yet.

j I ____________________ (not hear) anything from the doctor.

Do you think that she ______________________ (forget) me?

2 Streiche die falsche Alternative, *for* oder *since*, durch.

a Jack has been interested in history for/since a long time.

b We haven't played cards for/since last Christmas.

c Have you done anything interesting for/since I last saw you?

d Why me? You haven't taken the dog for a walk for/since weeks.

e My brother has watched TV all day for/since months.

f Ann has visited three museums for/since she's been here.

g I have had hundreds of emails for/since I won the lottery.

3 Vervollständige die Übersetzungen. Achte auf den unterschiedlichen Gebrauch des *simple present* und des *present perfect*.

a Die alte Frau wohnt in diesem Haus seit 67 Jahren.

The old woman ______________________ in this house

______________________________________.

b Ich mache meine Hausaufgaben, bevor ich irgendetwas anders tue.

I ______________________________________

______________________ anything else.

c Normalerweise gehen wir einkaufen am Wochenende.

We ______________________________________

______________________ weekend.

d Der Laden hat die Bücher immer noch nicht angeliefert.

The shop ______________________________________

______________________________________.

1
a Has the film started
b have not left
c has won
d have just switched on
e have you finished
f have not visited
g have not had
h Have you seen
i has Janna gone – has not written
j have not heard – has forgotten

2
a for a long time
b since last Christmas
c since I last saw you
d for weeks
e for months
f since she's been here
g since I won the lottery

3
a has lived, for 67 years
b do my homework before I do
c normally go shopping at the
d has still not delivered the books

30

Das *present perfect progressive*

Wir bilden das ***present perfect progressive*** mit *have/has* + *been* + *-ing*-Form des Vollverbs.
*I **have been waiting** to see the boss for nearly two hours.*
*Tom **has been talking** on the phone since 9 o'clock.*

Die **Verneinung** wird durch das Einfügen von *not/n't* unmittelbar nach dem Hilfsverb *have/has* gebildet.
*They **have not/haven't been working** here very long.*

Um **Fragen** zu bilden, tauschen wir das Hilfsverb *have/has* und das Subjekt einfach aus.
***Have** you **been watching** TV the whole afternoon?*

Wir benutzen das *present perfect progressive* für **länger andauernde,** zeitlich gestreckte **Handlungen** und **Situationen**, die in der Vergangenheit angefangen haben und **zum Zeitpunkt des Sprechens noch andauern.**

Im Deutschen benutzen wir in solchen Fällen meist das Präsens mit „schon", um zu verdeutlichen, dass die Handlung bereits länger andauert:
*I **have been waiting** for the bus since 2 o'clock.*
Ich warte schon seit 2 Uhr auf den Bus.

Diese Verben haben **keine** *progressive*-Form:
be, mean, believe, notice, dislike, see, hate, seem, know, want, like, wish, love

Überprüfe hier, ob das Wissen sitzt

Kreuze [x] die richtige Form an. Wähle die *progressive*-Form nur dann, wenn die Handlung eine ungewöhnlich lange Zeit angedauert hat. Sonst wähle die *simple*-Form.

a Tim has played [ ]/has been playing [ ] video games all weekend. Can that be good?

b I have tried [ ]/have been trying [ ] to get into the internet for hours.

c Jane has won [ ]/has been winning [ ] a prize for her photos.

d Ben has talked [ ]/has been talking [ ] non-stop for over an hour now. Nobody else has said [ ]/has been saying [ ] a word.

e I have not seen [ ]/have not been seeing [ ] that film yet. Let's go tonight, shall we?

f We have looked [ ]/have been looking for [ ] a second-hand digital camera for months now, but we have not found [ ]/have not been finding [ ] a good one yet.

g Barbara has invited [ ]/has been inviting [ ] dozens of people to her party next Saturday.

h It's not fair. Joshua has used [ ]/has been using [ ] the bathroom for hours now.

i Frank's a fool. The boss has spoken [ ]/has been speaking [ ] to him so often about his work and he has taken [ ]/has been taking [ ] no notice at all.

Richtig sind diese Formen:

a has been playing
b have been trying
c has won
d has been talking – has said
e have not seen
f have been looking for – have not found
g has invited
h has been using
i has spoken – has taken

31

Das *simple past*

Beim **simple past** unterscheiden wir zwischen **regelmäßigen** und **unregelmäßigen** Verben.
Bei den regelmäßigen Verben hängen wir bei allen Personen ein *-ed* an den Infinitiv an.
*Our team **played** very well last Saturday.*

Die **unregelmäßigen Verben** dagegen haben eine besondere Form, die man sich einfach merken muss.
*Tom **bought** a new bike yesterday.*

Beim Anhängen von *-ed* gibt es folgende Schreibregeln:
Ein stummes (= nicht ausgesprochenes) *-e* fällt weg:

bake → *bak**ed***
live → *liv**ed***
move → *mov**ed***
phone → *phon**ed***

Das *-y* nach einem Konsonanten wird zum *-i*:

*carr**y*** → *carr**ied***
*hurr**y*** → *hurr**ied***
*tr**y*** → *tr**ied***

Endet dagegen das Verb auf *-y* nach einem Vokal, bleibt das *-y* unverändert:

*enjo**y*** → *enjo**yed***
*pla**y*** → *pla**yed***

Mit Ausnahme von *-x* wird ein Endkonsonant nach einem einfachen Vokal verdoppelt:

*be**g*** → *be**gg**ed*
*cla**p*** → *cla**pp**ed*
*fi**t*** → *fi**tt**ed*
*prefe**r*** → *prefe**rr**ed*
*ro**b*** → *ro**bb**ed*
*trave**l*** → *trave**ll**ed*

Ist kein Hilfsverb im Satz vorhanden, bilden wir die **Verneinung** mit *did not (didn't)*. Das Vollverb steht dabei immer im Infinitiv.
*I **did not/didn't go** to school last week. I was ill.*

Für **Fragen** gilt folgendes: Gibt es kein Hilfsverb im Satz, werden Fragen ebenfalls mit *did* gebildet.
***Did** you **see** that funny man?*

Bei Fragen mit *what?* und *who?* verfahren wir anders. Ist *what?* bzw. *who?* das **Subjekt** des Satzes, dann benötigen wir kein Hilfsverb, um Fragen zu bilden:
***What happened** on your way home yesterday?*
***Who taught** you English last year?*

Ist aber das Fragewort das **Objekt** des Satzes, dann bilden wir Fragen mit einem Hilfsverb, also wie gewöhnlich:
***What did you watch** on TV yesterday?*
***Who did you invite** to your party last Saturday?*

Wir benutzen das *simple past*, um **völlig abgeschlossene Handlungen in der Vergangenheit** zu schildern.

Das **simple past** tritt häufig mit den folgenden Zeitangaben auf:
yesterday, the day before yesterday, the other day (neulich)
two/three/four/... days/weeks/months/... ago
last night/week/month/...
last January/spring/Christmas/...
in 2007/...
at this/that time (zu dieser/jener Zeit), in those days (damals)
when he was a boy, when she went to school ...

Überprüfe hier, ob das Wissen sitzt

1 Benutze das *simple past.* Achte auf die vielen unregelmäßigen Verben.

a Last Saturday, a big new shopping mall ________ (open) near Dublin.

b The mall __________ (be) huge. It _________ (have) over 150 shops, restaurants and cinemas.

c On opening day, some shops _______ (try) to attract customers with free gifts.

d For example, if you _____________ (buy) a computer, you ______ (get) a free printer with it.

e One travel agent _______ (sell) two-week holidays in Spain with one week free.

f Of course, the Galloways all _______ (go) to the opening of the mall.

g Mr Galloway ____________ (park) the car in a big car park and then they ____________ (catch) the shuttle bus to the mall. The car park and the shuttle ___________________ (not cost) anything, of course.

h As they _____________________ (not want) to go to the same shops, they _______________ (arrange) to meet at the shuttle bus at 4 pm.

i Mr and Mrs Galloway ____________ (arrive) there on time, but where ________ (be) their teenagers, Kathleen and Kevin? Shuttles ________ (come) and shuttles ________ (go), but they still ________ ________ (not show) up.

j After nearly an hour, Mr and Mrs Galloway ___________ (begin) to get worried because Kathleen and Kevin ______________ (not be) normally late.

2 Benutze die Satzelemente, um Fragen mit dem *simple past* zu bilden. Einige Wörter müssen hinzugefügt werden.

a where/you + be/all this time/?

____

b you + have/good time/?

____

c Kathleen + buy/nice bag/?

____

d Kevin + go/a phone shop/?

____

e they + eat/a burger bar/?

____

f when/they + get home/?

____

g what/happen/mall/?

____

h what/teenagers + say/?

____

1
a opened
b was – had
c tried
d bought – got
e sold
f went
g parked – caught – did not cost
h did not want – arranged
i arrived – were – came – went – did not show
j began – were not

2
a Where were you all this time?
b Did you have a good time?
c Did Kathleen buy a nice bag?
d Did Kevin go to a phone shop?
e Did they eat at a burger bar?
f When did they get home?
g What happened at the mall?
h What did the teenagers say?

32

Das *past progressive*

Wir bilden das **past progressive** mit *was/were* + *-ing*-Form des Vollverbs.
*We **were playing** football at 3 o'clock yesterday.*
*I **was cleaning** the house all day last Monday.*
*When Tom arrived they **were having** lunch.*

Da beim *past progressive* immer ein Hilfsverb – *was/were* – vorhanden ist, wird die **Verneinung** einfach mit *not/n't* gebildet.
*Ben **was not/wasn't working** when I saw him.*

Um **Fragen** zu bilden, tauschen wir *was/were* und das Subjekt einfach aus.
***Were** the police **stopping** all cars?*

Möchten wir ausdrücken, dass eine **Handlung** zu einem bestimmten Zeitpunkt oder während eines bestimmten Zeitraumes in der **Vergangenheit im Gange** (= *in progress)* **war,** benutzen wir das *past progressive.*

Wollen wir verdeutlichen, dass eine **Handlung schon im Gange** war, als ein **neues Ereignis** (plötzlich) eintrat, verwenden wir ebenfalls das *past progressive.*

Einige Verben haben keine *progressive*-Form (siehe Seite 87, 94).

Überprüfe hier, ob das Wissen sitzt

Streiche die falsche Alternative durch.

a It was/was being about six o'clock on a Friday evening. Mark's mother cooked/was cooking when the phone suddenly rang/was ringing.

b The caller was/was being John Davis from the phone shop in Victoria Road.

c "I'm sorry, Mrs Parks," he said/was saying, "but one of our customers just caught/was catching your son Mark as he left/was leaving the shop without paying for an expensive mobile phone."

d At first, Mark's mother did not worry/was not worrying.

e She thought/was thinking it was/was being all a terrible mistake.

f "I know my son," she told/was telling Mr Davis. "There's no way that Mark would ever steal anything."

g "I wish that was/was being true," he replied/was replying, "but it's clear what happened/was happening.

h Our other customer watched/was watching Mark the whole time, although he did not know/was not knowing that, of course.

i He put/was putting the phone into his pocket while the assistant, Julia, helped/was helping somebody else. Then he started/was starting to leave the shop.

j Our customer followed/was following him as he walked/was walking out of the shop and stopped/was stopping him just outside in the street.

a was – was cooking – rang
b was
c said – caught – was leaving
d did not worry
e thought – was
f told
g was – replied – happened
h was watching – did not know
i put – was helping – started
j followed – was walking – stopped

33

Das *past perfect*

Wir bilden das **past perfect** mit *had* + Partizip Perfekt (3. Form). Die Form ist bei allen Personen die gleiche.
When we arrived at the cinema, the film ***had started.***

Bei **regelmäßigen Verben** hat das Partizip Perfekt (3. Form) dieselbe Form wie das *simple past*, also Infinitiv + *-ed*.

Bei **unregelmäßigen Verben** dagegen hat das Partizip Perfekt eine besondere Form, die man sich einfach merken muss.
By the time the police came the thieves ***had driven away.***

Die **Verneinung** wird durch das Einfügen von *not/n't* unmittelbar nach dem Hilfsverb *had* gebildet.
They ***had not/hadn't finished*** *the lunch when I phoned.*

Um **Fragen** zu bilden, tauschen wir das Hilfsverb *had* und das Subjekt einfach aus.
Had *the train* ***left*** *when you got to the station?*

Wir benutzen das *past perfect,* um zu verdeutlichen, dass eine **Handlung in der Vergangenheit bereits abgeschlossen war,** als eine andere Handlung anfing.

Zum Vergleich:
When we arrived at school, lessons ***began.*** *(simple past)*
Als wir zur Schule kamen, begann der Unterricht.

When we arrived at school, lessons ***had (already) begun.*** *(past perfect)*
Als wir zur Schule kamen, hatte der Unterricht (bereits) begonnen.

Überprüfe hier, ob das Wissen sitzt

Setze das *simple past* oder das *past perfect* in die Sätze ein. Benutze das *past perfect* mit den unterstrichenen Verben.

a Can the witness tell us whether the fight __________ (begin) when he ___________ (arrive), or whether it ___________________ (already + start) when he _____ (get) there.

b Tragically, the accident victim ______________________ (already + die) by the time the ambulance ____________ (reach) the hospital.

c By the time we _________ (find) our seats, the concert __________ (begin).

d After I _____________ (read) that Sara Connors _______ (be) in the film, I ____________ (decide) to go and see it.

e When Mum _______ (ring) the school this morning, the teacher she ____________ (want) to speak to _____________ (go) home.

f Before we _______ (take) Ben to the theatre, he ____________ ___________ (never/see) a live performance before.

g I _______________________ (just/change) into some clean jeans when the dog _____________ (jump up) and _________ (make) them dirty.

a began – arrived – already started – got
b had already died – reached
c found – had begun
d had read – was – decided
e rang – wanted – had gone
f took – had never seen
g had just changed – jumped up – made

34

Das *past perfect progressive*

Wir bilden das **past perfect progressive** mit *had* + *been* + *-ing*-Form des Vollverbs. Die Form ist für alle Personen gleich.

I had been sitting *in the train for an hour before it left the station.*

The workers ***had been striking*** *for a month by the time they got more money.*

Die **Verneinung** wird durch das Einfügen von *not/n't* unmittelbar nach dem Hilfsverb *had* gebildet.

We ***had not/hadn't been waiting*** *long before the teacher arrived.*

Um **Fragen** zu bilden, tauschen wir das Hilfsverb *had* und das Subjekt einfach aus.

Had *you* ***been living*** *in London long when you bought your house?*

Wir benutzen das *past perfect progressive,* um zu sagen, dass eine in der Vergangenheit begonnene Handlung bis zu einem **bestimmten Zeitpunkt in der Vergangenheit** andauerte.

Überprüfe hier, ob das Wissen sitzt

Unterstreiche alle Zeitformen des *simple past,* rahme alle Zeitformen des *past perfect* ein und setze eine gestrichelte Linie unter alle Formen des *past perfect progressive.*

Bob Potter was worried. He and his wife Wendy wanted to go to Croatia on holiday. Bob had spent the whole morning searching for his passport, but he had not found it anywhere.

While Bob had been looking for his passport, Wendy had been working hard, too. She had cooked a wonderful meal. She had made vegetable soup and a delicious meat pie, which she had baked in the oven.

But although Bob normally loved his food, he didn't enjoy his meal much. "What's the matter, Bob?" Wendy asked. Then Bob told her that he had lost his passport.

When she heard this, Wendy had laughed. "Your passport? Oh, I've got that. I found it in the oven." Then Bob remembered. He had hidden his passport in the oven so that he wouldn't lose it.

simple past	past perfect	past perfect progressive
was (worried)	had spent	had been looking for
wanted	had not found	had been working
loved	had cooked	
didn't enjoy	had made	
asked	had baked	
told	had lost	
heard	had laughed	
found	had hidden	
remembered		

35

Das Futur mit *will*

Das **Futur mit *will*** bilden wir mit *will* + Infinitiv des Vollverbs. Es hat für alle Personen die gleiche Form.
In future good qualifications ***will become*** *more and more important.*
I'm sure the EU ***will grow*** *closer together.*
We think that Tom and Sally ***will marry*** *soon.*

Die **Verneinung** wird durch das Einfügen von *not* unmittelbar nach *will* gebildet.
Of course Britain ***will not/won't leave*** *the EU.*

Beachte die Kurzform *won't (= will not).*

Um **Fragen** zu bilden, tauschen wir *will* und das Subjekt einfach aus.
Oh, dear. It's raining. ***Will*** *you* ***lend*** *me your umbrella?*

Wir benutzen das *will*-Futur für
- zukünftige Situationen/Ereignisse, die mit Sicherheit eintreten werden,
- Erwartungen, Vermutungen und Hoffnungen,
- spontane, vorher nicht überlegte Entscheidungen.

Daher tritt das Futur mit *will* mit den folgenden einleitenden **Verben** besonders häufig auf:

to believe	(glauben)
to hope	(hoffen)
to imagine	(hier: glauben)
to suppose	(vermuten)
to think	(denken, meinen)

Überprüfe hier, ob das Wissen sitzt

Benutze das Futur mit *will,* um die Sätze aus einer Wettervorhersage zu vervollständigen.

a You ________________ (not need) your umbrella in south-east England tomorrow because the weather __________ (be) dry and you ______________ (enjoy) plenty of sunshine.

b Unfortunately, you ________________ (not have) so much luck in the south-west. Here it __________ (be) cloudy in the morning and rain ______________ (move) in from the Atlantic later in the day. With the rain, it __________________ (become) increasingly windy.

c In fact, this _______________ (apply) to all western parts of Britain, where it ____________ (rain) and temperatures ____________ (fall). However, these wet and chilly *(kühl)* conditions ________________ (not last) long. Tomorrow, the clouds _______________________ (disappear) and the sun ______________ (come) out.

d And what ______________________________ (the weather/be) like in the rest of England and Scotland? Well, the eastern side of the UK ______________ (not see) much sunshine, I'm afraid, but it _______ __________________ (at least + stay) dry. And you ______________ (have) light winds and average temperatures, too.

a won't need – will be – will enjoy
b won't have – will be – will move – will become
c will apply – will rain – will fall – won't last – will disappear – will come
d will the weather be – won't see – will at least stay – will have

Das Futur mit *going to*

Das **Futur** mit ***going to*** bilden wir mit *am/is/are* + *going to* + Infinitiv des Vollverbs.

*Helen **is going to buy** a new bike.*
*Sally and Tom **are going to move** to London soon.*
*Look at the sky. It **is going to snow.***

Beachte: *Going to* und der Infinitiv bleiben bei allen Personen unverändert.

Die **Verneinung** wird durch das Einfügen von *not* unmittelbar nach *am/is/are* gebildet.
*I **am not going to look for** a job until after my holiday.*

Um **Fragen** zu bilden, tauschen wir *am/is/are* und das Subjekt einfach aus.
***Are** you **going to invite** Helen to your party?*

Wir benutzen das Futur mit *going to* für **zukünftige Pläne** und **Absichten.**

Wir verwenden das Futur mit *going to* auch für Ereignisse und Situationen, **die bald eintreten werden.** Dies ist besonders der Fall, wenn im Augenblick des Sprechens eindeutige Anzeichen dafür bereits gegeben sind.

Überprüfe hier, ob das Wissen sitzt

Benutze die richtige Form des *will-* oder *going to-*Futurs.

a I'm sure Ann ______________________ (enjoy) her holiday.

b The Greens ______________________ (fly) to Florida this year.

c Sarah says she ______________________ (learn) French in the autumn.

d The Austrians ______________________ (ban) snowboarders from some slopes.

e The police say that people __________________ (not obey) a lower speed limit.

f The tourists __________ (be) disappointed, but the forecast says we ________________ (not have) any new snow this week.
Really? We __________________ (have to) get a snow-making machine.
Yes, but where ______________________________ (we/find) one?

g We ____________ (have) problems if there are any more accidents.
I know, but what ________________________ (we/do) about it?

h Tom says he ______________________ (book) a holiday on the internet. He thinks he ____________ (save) a lot of money that way.

a will enjoy
b are going to fly
c is going to learn
d are going to ban
e will not obey
f will be – will not have – will have to – are we going to find
g will have – are we going to do
h is going to book – will save

Zeiten des Präsens mit zukünftiger Bedeutung

Das *simple present*

Das ***simple present* mit zukünftiger Bedeutung** tritt immer mit einer geeigneten Zeitangabe der zukünftigen Zeit auf.

My train ***leaves at 3.35 pm on Sunday.***

I can't come until 4. I ***have a piano lesson next Friday.***

Don't forget the film ***starts at 7.30 tomorrow.***

Genau wie im Deutschen benutzen wir auch im Englischen das *simple present* mit einer adverbialen Bestimmung der Zeit, um **fest terminierte Vorgänge** (Fahrpläne, Stundenpläne, Programme usw.) anzugeben.

Das *present progressive*

Das ***present progressive* mit zukünftiger Bedeutung** tritt immer mit einem Adverb der zukünftigen Zeit auf.

We ***are giving*** *a party* ***at the weekend.***

Tom ***is not/isn't leaving*** *school* ***in July.***

Are *you* ***going*** *to the football match* ***on Saturday?***

In dieser Bedeutung benutzen wir das *present progressive*, um **schon entschiedene Pläne** und **Verabredungen** auszudrücken.

Überprüfe hier, ob das Wissen sitzt

1 Bilde Sätze mit dem *going to*-Futur oder dem *present progressive*. Benutze das *present progressive* nur dann, wenn es ein Adverb der zukünftigen Zeit gibt. Einige Wörter müssen hinzugefügt werden.

a I/buy/new skis/Austria

____

b Tom/fly/USA/next Saturday

____

c Sarah/collect/tickets/travel agent's/tomorrow

____

2 Setze die Verben in die richtige Form des *will*-Futurs, *going to*-Futurs, *present progressive* oder *simple present*.

a What time ______________ (film/start) tomorrow, Ann?
It ________ (begin) at 8, but we ______________ (meet) in the café at 7.

b ______________________ (Alan/give up) football?
No. He ______________ (play) in the match on Saturday.

c We ______________ (not go) away on holiday at all next summer. We ______________ (spend) the whole time at home.

d The weather forecast says that it ________ (be) sunny at the weekend. ______________ (you/come) cycling with us?
I don't know. I ______________ (tell) you tomorrow, okay?

1 a I am going to buy new skis in Austria.
b Tom is flying to the USA next Saturday.
c Sarah is collecting the tickets from the travel agent's tomorrow.

2 a does the film start – begins – are meeting
b Is Alan going to give up – is playing
c are not going – are spending
d will be – Will you come – will tell

Das *future progressive*

Wir bilden das ***future progressive*** mit *will be* + *-ing*-Form des Vollverbs. Die Form ist bei allen Personen gleich.
*I **will be earning** more money soon.*
*This time next year she **will be visiting** her parents in Chicago.*

Die **Verneinung** wird durch das Einfügen von *not* unmittelbar nach *will* gebildet.
*In future, people **will not/won't be keeping** the same job for the whole of their working life.*

Um **Fragen** zu bilden, tauschen wir *will* und das Subjekt einfach aus.
***Will** you **be spending** all your time in the office from now on?*

Wir benutzen das *future progressive* für **andauernde Situationen** und **Handlungen in der Zukunft.**

Überprüfe hier, ob das Wissen sitzt

Bilde das *future progressive.* Achte auf verneinten Aussagen und Fragen.

a What ______________________ (do) this time next week?
I ______________ (fly) to Cape Town where I __________ __________ (meet) my friend, Frank Webb.

b Thank heavens, we __________________ (not sit) in this office tomorrow. We ______________________ (get ready) to go on holiday.

c I want to send Anna a message. ____________________ (you/see) her this weekend?
Sorry. I __________________ (not see) her before the end of the month.

d The nicest thing about a holiday is the anticipation *(Vorfreude).* In a few weeks, we __________________ (relax) by the pool. You ______________________ (sunbathe) and I __________ ______ (lie) under a sun umbrella with a good book. And one thing is sure: we ______ ______________________ (definitely + not think) about work.

a will you be doing – will be flying – will be meeting
b won't be sitting – will be getting ready
c Will you be seeing – won't be seeing
d will be relaxing – will be sunbathing – will be lying – will definitely not be thinking

TESTEN • TESTEN • TESTEN • TESTEN • TESTEN • TESTEN • TESTEN

Das *future perfect*

Wir bilden das ***future perfect*** mit *will have* + Partizip Perfekt (3. Form). Die Form ist dieselbe für alle Personen.
*You can collect the car at 5. The mechanic **will have repaired** it by then.*

Bei **regelmäßigen Verben** hat das Partizip Perfekt dieselbe Form wie die des *simple past*, also Infinitiv + *-ed*.
*I'm sorry, but can you come back in an hour? We **will not/won't have finished** your car before 6.*

Die **unregelmäßigen Verben** dagegen haben eine besondere Form, die man sich einfach merken muss.
***Will** Susan **have done** her exams by the end of July?*

Die **Verneinung** wird durch das Einfügen von *not* unmittelbar nach *will* gebildet.

Beachte die Kurzform *won't (= will not).*

Um **Fragen** zu bilden, tauschen wir *will* und das Subjekt einfach aus.

Wir benutzen das *future perfect,* wenn eine Handlung zu einem gegebenen Zeitpunkt **in der Zukunft abgeschlossen** sein wird.

Das *future perfect* wird häufig mit bestimmten **Zeitangaben** benutzt.
Dazu gehören:
by Christmas
before next July
until August
by the end of next year

Überprüfe hier, ob das Wissen sitzt

1 Benutze das *future perfect*. Achte auf verneinte Aussagen und Fragen.

a They ______________________ (paint) the door by the time we get home.

b ______________________ (Ben/finish) the report by lunchtime?

c I ______________________ (not fix) the TV by the time the film begins.

d ______________________ (we/arrive) in Dover by breakfast?

e They ______________________ (not return) home by ten.

2 Schreibe die Futurformen mit den angegebenen Ersatzverben wie in den beiden Beispielen um.

Will you have a dance? (would like) → Would you like a dance?

I am going to take a day off (plan) → I plan to take a day off.

a What will you do now? (mean)

______________________ now?

b I won't do what you want. (refuse)

I ______________________ what you want.

c I'm going to find a new job. (intend)

______________________ a new job.

d We will definitely be there. (promise)

______________________ to be there.

1 a will have painted
b Will Ben have finished
c will not have fixed
d Will we have arrived
e will not have returned

2 a What do you mean to do
b refuse to do
c I intend to find
d We promise

40

Das deutsche Verb „lassen" auf Englisch

Im Deutschen hat das Verb „lassen" mehrere Bedeutungen, die im Englischen mit verschiedenen Verben ausgedrückt werden müssen.

- Bedeutet „lassen" **„zulassen"** oder **„erlauben"**, benutzen wir im Englischen die Muster:
  (not) let + Objekt + Infinitiv ohne *to (not let us go)*
  (not) allow + Objekt + *to*-Infinitiv *(allows me to stay up)*
  *Mrs Adams **didn't let us go** home early.*
  *My dad **allows me to stay up** as long as I want.*

- Wird „lassen" im Sinne von **„veranlassen"** oder **„jemanden zwingen, etwas zu tun"** gebraucht, benutzen wir im Englischen:
  make + Objekt + Infinitiv ohne *to (made Ben finish)* oder verstärkt:
  force + Objekt + *to*-Infinitiv *(forced the pilot to land)*
  *Tom **made Ben finish** the report before lunch.*
  *The hijacker **forced the pilot to land.***

- „Lassen" in der Bedeutung von **„etwas erledigen/machen lassen"** wird im Englischen ausgedrückt mit:
  have + Objekt + Partizip Perfekt (3. Form) *(will have the car repaired).*
  In der **Umgangssprache** können wir *get* statt *have* benutzen *(did you get delivered).*
  *I'**ll have the car repaired** immediately.*
  ***Did** you **get the meal delivered** or did you cook it?*

Überprüfe hier, ob das Wissen sitzt

Ergänze die englischen Formen für das deutsche Verb „lassen“. Benutze die Formen, die jeweils oben drüber angegeben sind.

let + Objekt + Infinitiv ohne *to*

a My parents ______________________ as long as I want.
(*lassen mich aufbleiben*)

b Mrs Bond ______________________ yesterday.
(*ließ ihre Klasse fernsehen)*

c Our teachers ______________________ in the dictionary in tests. (*lassen uns nicht Wörter ... nachschlagen)*

make + Objekt + Infinitiv ohne *to*

d The doctor ______________________ some medicine.
(*ließ mich ... einnehmen)*

e The bank robbers ______________________ . (*ließen uns hinlegen)*

f ______________________ mistakes?
(*Lässt Mrs Bond euch ... verbessern)*

have/get + Objekt + Partizip Perfekt

g I hope Dad ______________________ soon.
(*den Rekorder reparieren lässt)*

h They ______________________ .
(*das Gras immer noch nicht schneiden lassen)*

a let me stay up
b let her class watch TV
c don't let us look up words
d made me take
e made us lie down
f Does Mrs Bond make you correct
g has/gets the recorder fixed
h have still not had/got the grass cut

Modale Hilfsverben (Merkmale)

Möchten wir sagen, was geschehen **kann, muss, darf, soll** usw., benutzen wir ein **modales Hilfsverb** in Verbindung mit einem Vollverb. Das Hilfsverb wird immer mit dem **Infinitiv des Vollverbs ohne *to*** verwendet:
*You **can go** home now.*
*You **must finish** your homework.*
*The girls **may watch** TV now.*
*Josh **should go** to the dentist's.*

Anders als im Deutschen steht das Hilfsverb **nie ohne Vollverb:**
*Tom **can speak** German.* Tom kann Deutsch.
*I **must go** now.* Ich muss jetzt weg.
***May I go** to the cinema?* Darf ich ins Kino?
*You **should not do** that!* Das solltest du nicht!

Modale Hilfsverben haben bei allen Personen die gleiche Form. Anders als bei Vollverben hat die 3. Person Singular *(he/she/it)* **keine *s*-Endung:**
***She can** play the piano very well.*
***He must** work harder.*

Wie bei den Hilfsverben *be, have* und *do* bilden wir die **Verneinung** und **Fragen** ohne *do/does/did:*
*Bob **cannot dance.***
***Can Lars speak** English?*

Mit Ausnahme von *may* und *might* können wir die **Verneinung** mit *n't (not)* abkürzen:
***Couldn't** you ask your teacher?*
*You **mustn't** (must not) eat during lessons.*
aber:
*We **may not** go home yet.*
*They **might not** come to the party.*

Wir können die modalen Hilfsverben **nur im Präsens** und **mit zukünftiger Bedeutung** gebrauchen:

*You **can watch** TV now.*	Präsens
*We **can visit** you next Friday.*	Zukunft

*I **must do** my homework now.* Präsens
*I **must wash** the car tomorrow.* Zukunft

*Mr Grey says we **may go** home now.* Präsens
*Sally **may go** to the USA next summer.* Zukunft

*You **should clean** your teeth twice a day.* Präsens
*They **should arrive** home next Saturday.* Zukunft

Möchten wir ein modales Hilfsverb z. B. in der **Vergangenheit** *(past)* benutzen, müssen wir ein geeignetes **Ersatzverb** *(substitute)* einsetzen:
*I **had to walk** to school this morning.*
*We **weren't allowed to watch** TV yesterday.*
*Josh **wasn't able to play** football last Saturday.*

Gebrauch	Modale Hilfsverben
Fähigkeit *(ability)*	*I can swim.* Ich kann schwimmen.
Möglichkeit *(possibility)*	*It could/may/might rain later.* Später könnte es regnen.
Bitte *(request)*	*Can/May I open a window?* Kann/Darf ich ein Fenster öffnen?
Erlaubnis *(permission)*	*You **can/may** watch TV now.* Jetzt kannst/darfst du fernsehen.
Verbot *(ban)*	*You **mustn't** be late.* Du darfst nicht zu spät sein.
Pflicht *(obligation)*	*You **must** learn these words.* Du musst diese Wörter lernen.
Wahl *(free choice)*	*You **needn't** make the beds.* Du musst nicht die Betten machen.
Empfehlung *(recommendation)*	*You **should/ought to** see a doctor.* Du solltest einen Arzt aufsuchen.

Überprüfe hier, ob das Wissen sitzt

1 Vervollständige die Sätze mit englischen Entsprechungen der deutschen Ausdrücke wie im Beispiel.

Nowadays, you ... bikes at coffee shops. *(kaufen können)*
Nowadays, you can buy bikes at coffee shops.

a People ______________________________ their mobiles in buses.
(ausschalten sollen)

b I ______________________________ to my parents today.
(schreiben müssen)

c Anybody ______________________________ a foreign language.
(lernen können)

d Pedestrians ______________________________ this road on weekdays.
(nicht benutzen dürfen)

e ______________________________ this DVD?
(ich/ausleihen dürfen)

f I'm afraid I ______________________________ German.
(nicht verstehen können)

2 Vervollständige die Sätze mit dem richtigen modalen Hilfsverb.

a You ______________________ (not use) a mobile phone in cinemas.
(Verbot)

b ______________________ (I/borrow) your scooter, please, Julie?
(höfliche Bitte)

c Sarah said that he ________________ (use) her phone to ring home.
(Erlaubnis)

d In a few years, emails ______________ (mean) people won't write letters at all.
(Möglichkeit)

e You ______________ (arrive) on time or they won't let you in.
(Verpflichtung)

f You ______________ (send) emails if you don't want to. You can always send a text message instead.
(freie Wahl)

1 a should switch off
b must write
c can learn
d must not use
e May I borrow
f cannot understand

2 a must not use
b May I borrow
c could use
d may mean
e must arrive
f need not send

42

Can/could, be able to, be allowed to

Wie bei dem deutschen Modalverb „können“, benutzen wir *can*, um **Fähigkeit, Erlaubnis** und **Bitten** auszudrücken.
*Helen **can drive** a car.*
*You **can watch** the late movie.*
***Can** I **close** the window, please?*

Möchten wir eine **Möglichkeit** ausdrücken, benutzen wir (neben anderen Formulierungen) *could:*
*Be careful. You **could fall.***

Sprechen wir über eine **Fähigkeit** in der **Vergangenheit**, benutzen wir ebenfalls *could*.
*Tom **could speak** German when he was six.*

Möchten wir jedoch eine **Erlaubnis** in der **Vergangenheit** ausdrücken, benutzen wir das Ersatzverb *was/were allowed to:*
*We **were allowed to watch** the late movie yesterday.*

Um über etwas in der **Zukunft** zu sprechen, können wir entweder *can* benutzen mit zukünftiger Bedeutung oder die Ersatzverben *will be able to* (Fähigkeit) und *will be allowed to* (Erlaubnis).
*I **can't come** before 10 tomorrow.*
*I **won't be able to come** before 10 tomorrow.*
***Can** we **go** home early next Friday?*
***Will** we **be allowed to go** home early next Friday?*

Die Verben *be able to* und *be allowed to* können auch in der Gegenwart und der Vergangenheit benutzt werden.

Überprüfe hier, ob das Wissen sitzt

Setze *can/can't* oder *could/couldn't* ein. Benutze Wörter aus dem Kasten, um den Gebrauch anzugeben, und streiche sie dann durch.

Bitte	Möglichkeit	Fähigkeit	Erlaubnis
Erlaubnis	~~Fähigkeit~~	höfliche Bitte	

a I *can* ________ come to your party next Saturday.
Fähigkeit ________

b ________ you help me with my homework, please? ________

c We ________ go home until we've finished this job.
____

d Cars ________ park free in P+R car parks.
____

e We ________ find a cheap hotel anywhere last July.
____

f I suppose I ________ help you tomorrow, but not for long. ________

g ________ you spell your name for me, please. ________

b Can, Bitte
c can't, Erlaubnis
d can, Erlaubnis
e couldn't, Fähigkeit
f could, Möglichkeit
g Could, höfliche Bitte
Die Antworten b und g können auch getauscht werden.

43

Must/have to, needn't/not have to, mustn't

	Gebrauch	Bedeutung
must	Zwang: *You **must give back** books after 14 days.* dringende Notwendigkeit: *People **must protect** nature.* Schlussfolgerung: *You **must be** mad to drink and drive.*	müssen
needn't	kein Zwang; keine Notwendigkeit: *We **needn't go** to school today.*	nicht brauchen, nicht müssen
mustn't	Verbot: *You **mustn't drive** faster than 30 kph here.*	nicht dürfen

Wir benutzen das Modalverb *must* nur im Präsens.

Möchten wir über die **Zukunft** reden, können wir entweder *must* mit zukünftiger Bedeutung oder das Ersatzverb *will have to* benutzen.
*Helen **must/will have to go** to the dentist's soon.*

Wollen wir über die **Vergangenheit** reden, verwenden wir das Ersatzverb *had to.*
*I **had to go** home early yesterday.*

Achtung Fehlerquelle: Die **Verneinung** von *must* ist *needn't* (wird also auf keinen Fall mit *must* gebildet).

Wir können das Problem mit *must* bzw. *needn't* sehr leicht vermeiden, indem wir immer *have to* bzw. *not have to* benutzen:
*I **must/have to go** to the dentist's.*
*You **needn't/don't have to** do this exercise.*

Überprüfe hier, ob das Wissen sitzt

1 Benutze *must, mustn't* oder *needn't* mit den Vollverben.

a You ____________________ write an email. Send a text message instead.

b Kevin thinks he __________________ wear designer clothes just to impress people.

c That sign means that you ________________________ ever stop here.

d We _________________ leave now or we'll miss the start of the film.

2 Schreibe die Sätze aus Übung 1 mit *have to/not have to* um. Welcher Satz kann nicht umgeschrieben werden, und warum?

a You ___________________________________ write an email. Send a text message instead.

b Kevin thinks he __________________________ wear designer clothes just to impress people.

c That sign means that you ___________________________________ ever stop here.

d We ______________________________ leave now or we'll miss the start of the film.

Satz _______ kann nicht mit *have to* umgeschrieben werden, weil er ein ____________________________________ ausdrückt.

1 a needn't write
b must wear
c mustn't ever stop
d must leave

2 a don't have to write
b has to wear
c mustn't ever stop
d have to leave

Satz c) kann nicht mit *have to* umgeschrieben werden, weil er ein (absolutes) Verbot ausdrückt.

44

May/might und *should/ought to*

■ *May/might*

Wir benutzen *may,* um **Möglichkeit, Erlaubnis** und **höfliche Bitten** auszudrücken.

A lot of people ***may lose*** *their jobs.*
You ***may see*** *the doctor now.*
May *I* ***speak*** *to Mr Adams, please?*

Wollen wir eine **entferntere Möglichkeit** oder eine **extrem höfliche Bitte** ausdrücken, können wir *might* benutzen.

We ***might see*** *each other on Saturday.*
Might *I* ***have*** *another cup of tea, please?*

■ *Should/ought to*

Die Modalverben *should* und *ought to* entsprechen dem deutschen Modalverb „sollten".

Should und *ought to* haben die gleiche Bedeutung. Wir benutzen sie, um eine **Empfehlung** auszudrücken.

You ***should stop/ought to stop*** *smoking, Tom.*
We ***should visit/ought to visit*** *old Mr Coe today.*

Wollen wir einer Empfehlung **zusätzlichen Nachdruck** verleihen, können wir *must* statt *should/ought to* verwenden.

You ***must work*** *harder, Brenda.*

Überprüfe hier, ob das Wissen sitzt

Setze *may/may not, might/might not* oder *should* gemäß dem angegebenen Gebrauch ein.

a ______________________ I open a window, please?

höfliche Bitte

b We ______________________ see you there, but no promises.

entfernte Möglichkeit

c Frank ______________________ eat less and do more exercise.

Empfehlung

d You ______________________ go in to see the doctor now.

Erlaubnis

e Let's go early or we ______________________ get a good seat.

Möglichkeit

f ______________________ I give you some polite advice?

extrem höfliche Bitte

g What do you think? ______________________ I speak to Anna?

Empfehlung

h The police ______________________ not prosecute you.

entfernte Möglichkeit

a May I open
b might see
c should eat
d may go
e may not get
f Might I give
g Should I speak
h might not prosecute

Die Zeitformen des Passivs

*English **is spoken** all over the world.*
*This church **was built** nearly 800 years ago.*
*The post **has not/hasn't been delivered** yet.*
***Was** your computer **made** in the USA?*
*The bike **must be returned** by 6 o'clock.*

Is spoken, was built, has not been delivered usw. sind Formen des Passivs. Wir bilden das Passiv mit einer **Form von *be* und der 3. Form (dem Partizip Perfekt) des Vollverbs.**

Zeit	Form von *be*	3. Form
simple present	*am/is/are*	*played*
present progressive	*am/is/are being*	*taught*
simple past	*was/were*	*stolen*
past progressive	*was/were being*	*decorated*
present perfect	*have/has been*	*lost*
past perfect	*had been*	*repaired*
will-Futur	*will be*	*opened*
going to-Futur	*am/is/are going to be*	*sent*

Da beim Passiv immer ein Hilfsverb (eine Form von *be*) vorhanden ist, wird die **Verneinung** mit *not/n't* gebildet.
Fragen werden durch die Umstellung von Subjekt und Hilfsverb gebildet.

Mit modalen Hilfsverben werden Passivsätze so gebildet:

Subjekt	Modalverb	*be*	3. Form	andere Teile
The bike	*must*	*be*	*returned*	*by 6.*
Drinks	*can*	*be*	*bought*	*at the kiosk.*
Cars	*should not*	*be*	*parked*	*here.*

Nach dem modalen Hilfsverb folgen der **Infinitiv von *be* (ohne *to!*) und die 3. Form (das Partizip Perfekt) des Vollverbs.**

Überprüfe hier, ob das Wissen sitzt

1 Setze die Verben in die richtige Form des Passivs ein. Benutze dabei das *simple present* oder das *simple past*.

a The Channel Tunnel __________________ (open) in 1994. The tunnel _______________ (make up) of two rail tunnels, one in each direction, that __________________ (separate) by a smaller service tunnel.

b The service tunnel, which ________________ (join) to the two rail tunnels every 375 metres, is a road tunnel that ____________ (use) by special vehicles.

c These vehicles __________________________ (drive) by electricity.

d The vehicle bodies ______________________ (can change) into ambulances, fire engines or buses in emergencies.

e This happened in November 1996, when one of the tunnels _______ ______________ (have to close) when a truck on a train caught fire.

f Some special vehicles _____________________ (change) into fire engines and others _______________ (use) as buses.

2 Vervollständige die Sätze mit Passivformen. Benutze immer ein modales Hilfsverb.

You can obtain advice about car security from the police.
Advice about car security can be obtained from the police.

a Drivers and passengers must wear seatbelts when the car is moving.

____ when the car is moving.

b You may not park cars on cycle tracks.

______________________________________ on cycle paths.

c You must activate some anti-theft systems with a spezial code.

____

____________________________________ with a special code.

d People should not hide expensive cameras unter seats.

____ under seats.

e You should never leave car papers in cars or thieves might steal them.

____ in cars or

____

f You may never lock dogs in cars during hot weather.

____

in cars during hot weather.

g Drivers should never position children's safety seats opposite airbags.

____

____________________________________ opposite airbags.

1
a was opened – is made up – are separated
b is joined – is used
c are driven
d can be changed
e had to be closed
f were changed – were used

2
a Seatbelts must be worn
b Cars may not be parked
c Some anti-theft systems must be activated
d Expensive cameras should not be hidden
e Car papers should never be left in cars or they might be stolen
f Dogs may never be locked
g Children's safety seats should never be positioned

TESTEN • TESTEN • TESTEN • TESTEN • TESTEN • TESTEN • TESTEN • TESTEN

46

Der Gebrauch des Passivs

Ist der **Verursacher** einer Handlung **unbekannt** oder **zweitrangig,** benutzen wir das Passiv. Die **Tat** – nicht also der Täter – steht im Vordergrund.
*The drugs **were found** in a London flat.*
*Police said they **had been imported** from Holland.*

Das Passiv kommt viel häufiger im Englischen als im Deutschen vor. Oft benutzen wir im Deutschen das Aktiv mit „man“, wenn im Englischen das Passiv verwendet wird:
*Valuables **can be given** in at the reception desk.*
Man kann Wertsachen an der Rezeption abgeben.

■ Das *by-agent*

Wollen wir den **Verursacher** eines Vorganges in einem Passivsatz angeben, benutzen wir einen ***by-agent.***
In der Regel wird der *by-agent* eine namentlich erwähnte **Person** bzw. **Gruppe** sein oder die **sachliche Ursache** des Vorganges darstellen.
*Tom Sawyer was written **by Mark Twain.***
*The first computers were built **by the Americans.***
*The fire was caused **by a cigarette.***

Der „Agent“ wird immer mit *by* – **auf keinen Fall** mit *from* – gebildet.

Überprüfe hier, ob das Wissen sitzt

Stelle die Aktivsätze ins Passivsätze um. Benutze einen *by-agent* nur, wenn er unbedingt notwendig ist.

a The Americans developed the computer chip.

b Somebody stole my bike last week.

c Tess Gerritsen didn't write this book.

d Visitors can buy guidebooks at the ticket office.

e Fossil fuels generate most of our electricity.

f People must switch off their mobile phones in hospitals.

a The computer chip was developed by the Americans.
b My bike was stolen last week.
c This book was not written by Tess Gerritsen.
d Guidebooks can be bought at the ticket office.
e Most of our electricity is generated by fossil fuels.
f Mobile phones must be switched off in hospitals.

Verben mit zwei Objekten und das unpersönliche Passiv

Verben mit zwei Objekten

1 *He sent her a postcard.* (Aktiv)
2 *She was sent a postcard.* (Passiv)

In Satz 1 hat das Verb *sent* zwei Objekte, ein **direktes Objekt** („wen oder was?") – *a postcard* – und ein **indirektes Objekt** („wem oder was?") – *her.* Ist der Verursacher unbekannt bzw. nicht so wichtig oder soll das indirekte Objekt betont werden, können wir einen Passivsatz bilden (Satz 2).

Dies erfolgt, indem das **indirekte Objekt** des Aktivsatzes *(her)* zum **Subjekt** des Passivsatzes *(she)* wird. Das **direkte Objekt** *(a postcard)* bleibt dabei als einziges Objekt des neuen Satzes erhalten.

Verben, die oft **zwei Objekte** haben, sind:
to ask, to give, to offer (anbieten), *to promise* (versprechen), *to send, to show* (zeigen), *to tell* (erzählen, mitteilen).

Das unpersönliche Passiv

It is said that *Britain might leave the EU.*
It was claimed that *two people died in the accident.*
It has been reported that *the school will be closed for years.*

Das Satzmuster *It is/was/has been* + 3. Form + *that* ... nennen wir das **unpersönliche Passiv.**
Wir benutzen das unpersönliche Passiv mit **Verben des Sagens und Denkens** wie *to believe* (glauben), *to claim* (behaupten), *to expect* (erwarten), *to fear* (befürchten), *to know, to report, to rumour* (munkeln), *to say* und *to think.*

Will der Sprecher sich möglichst **neutral** und **unbeteiligt** ausdrücken, kann er das unpersönliche Passiv verwenden. Daher kommt diese Struktur häufig in **Berichten** und **Gutachten** vor.

Überprüfe hier, ob das Wissen sitzt

1 Stelle die Sätze ins Aktiv bzw. Passiv wie im Beispiel.
Harry gave Wendy a kiss. → Wendy was given a kiss by Harry.

a I was asked the way by a driver.

____

b Carr & Co offered my brother a job.

____

c Julie promised Alan a date.

____

2 Schreibe die Sätze mit dem unpersönlichen Passiv um.
Almost all experts think that Arsenal will win the game.
It is thought by almost all experts that Arsenal will win the game.

a Somebody has claimed that the actor was drunk.

____

that the actor was drunk.

b People will believe that the government has something to hide.

__________________________________ that the government has something to hide.

c Most economists suggested that things must get better soon.

____

that things must get better soon.

1 a A driver asked me the way.
b My brother was offered a job by Carr & Co.
c Alan was promised a date by Julie.

2 a It has been claimed
b It will be believed
c It was suggested by most economists

48

Der Infinitiv und die *-ing*-Form nach bestimmten Verben

Häufig benutzen wir ein Verb – z. B. *hope, try, enjoy* und *like* – in Kombination mit anderen Verben.

Im Deutschen ist dies problemlos, da wir immer den Infinitiv verwenden:
*Ben **plans to go** to university.*
Ben **beabsichtigt,** die Universität **zu besuchen.**

*Some people **avoid paying** tax altogether.*
Einige Leute **vermeiden,** Steuern überhaupt **zu zahlen.**

Im Englischen dagegen benötigt eine Gruppe von Verben den **Infinitiv mit *to*** und eine andere Gruppe die ***-ing*-Form** (Gerundium).
*Tom and Helen **hope to go** on holiday soon.*
*I'll **try to phone** you at the weekend.*
*I **enjoy cycling** and **walking** very much.*
*Do you really **like watching** TV?*

Leider gibt es keine Regel, die die beiden Verbgruppen auf Anhieb bestimmt. Daher bleibt dir nichts anderes übrig, als die folgenden Listen auswendig zu lernen.

■ Verb + Infinitiv mit *to*

afford	*I can't afford to go on holiday.*	sich leisten
choose	*Jenny chose to stay single.*	wählen
decide	*He's decided to leave school.*	entscheiden
expect	*I expect to see Ben later.*	erwarten
hope	*Janna hopes to marry soon.*	hoffen
intend	*They intend to have a baby.*	beabsichtigen
mean	*I mean to ask for more money.*	etwas vorhaben
plan	*We plan to go away in May.*	planen
promise	*She promised to work harder.*	versprechen

refuse	*He refused to speak to me.*	verweigern
try	*They are trying to sell their car.*	versuchen
want	*We want to move to the USA.*	wollen

Verb + *-ing*-Form

admit	*He admits stealing the money.*	zugeben
avoid	*I avoid meeting him now.*	vermeiden
delay	*She delayed seeing a doctor.*	verschieben
deny	*He denies stealing the money.*	abstreiten
dislike	*I dislike dancing.*	nicht mögen
enjoy	*She enjoys going out.*	genießen
finish	*I've finished writing the email.*	beenden
hate	*They hate going to parties.*	hassen
imagine	*Imagine winning the lottery!*	sich vorstellen
keep	*He keeps hitting his dog.*	etwas dauernd tun
like	*I like listening to music.*	mögen
love	*We love meeting new people.*	sehr mögen
mention	*Did I mention seeing Susan?*	erwähnen
mind	*Do you mind being quieter?*	etwas dagegen haben
miss	*I missed seeing that film.*	versäumen
practise	*She often practises singing.*	üben
prefer	*I prefer eating at a restaurant.*	vorziehen
risk	*Don't risk losing the match.*	riskieren
suggest	*I suggest selling the house.*	vorschlagen

Überprüfe hier, ob das Wissen sitzt

1 Benutze die richtige Form des ersten Verbs und den *to*-Infinitiv bzw. die -*ing*-Form des zweiten. Siehe erst die Beispiellösungen an.
John admits **causing** (admit + cause) the accident.
I **meant to work** (mean + work) less last week, but I did more hours.

a We ______________________________
(cannot afford + go) on holiday this year.

b ______________________________
(Julie/choose + leave) school last July?

c It's terrible. They ______________________________
(keep + fight) all the time.

d Joshua ______________________________
(decide + get) a holiday job.

e Men often ______________________________
(delay + go) to the doctor's too long.

f Mandy ______________________________
(plan + get) a flat next May.

g ______________________________
(you/deny + lose) the car keys?

h Susan ______________________________
(not mention + meet) you in town.

i It's so hot. ______________________________
(you/mind + open) a window?

j I spoke to Jeff and he ______________________________
(promise + be) here on time.

k You ______________________________

(mustn't refuse + help) people in trouble.

l We ______________________________

(miss + see) the handball match yesterday.

m Barbara ______________________________

(practise + play) tennis every Wednesday.

2 Was ist richtig: *to*-Infinitiv oder die *-ing*-Form? Streiche die falsche Formulierung durch.

a We really enjoy travelling/to travel in the euro zone because we hate changing/to change money all the time. We think the UK should consider joining/to join the euro zone. I know this will mean giving up/to give up the pound, but so what?

b In 1973, the UK chose becoming/to become part of the EU. Now we should stop expecting/to expect special treatment and start taking/to take a full part in the union we joined. Or do we want risking/to risk isolating/to isolate ourselves? We really must avoid letting/to let that happen.

c My sister intends studying/to study American history so my dad suggested going/to go to a university in the USA. Anyhow, she has decided applying/to apply to Boston University and now she hopes starting/to start her course there next October.

1 a cannot afford to go
b Did Julie choose to leave
c keep fighting
d has decided to get
e delay going
f is planning to get
g Do you deny losing
h did not mention meeting
i Do you mind opening
j promised to be
k mustn't refuse to help
l missed seeing
m practises playing

2 a travelling – changing – joining – giving up
b to become – expecting – to take – to risk – isolating – letting
c to study – going – to apply – to start

Der Infinitiv oder die *-ing*-Form je nach Bedeutung

Bestimmte Verben können **je nach Bedeutung** mit der *-ing*-Form (Gerundium) oder mit dem *to*-Infinitiv verwendet werden.

■ ***forget, regret, remember***

*I'll never **forget meeting** my wife for the first time.*
Ich werde nie vergessen, wie ich meine Frau zum ersten Mal getroffen habe.

*Don't **forget to go** to the bank, please.*
Vergiss bitte nicht, zur Bank zu gehen.

*We **regret selling** the house but we need the money.*
Wir bedauern, unser Haus verkauft zu haben, aber wir brauchen das Geld.

*I **regret to tell** you that your dog died last night.*
Leider muss ich Ihnen mitteilen, dass Ihr Hund letzte Nacht gestorben ist.

*Do you **remember visiting** Istria in 2005?*
Erinnerst du dich, wie wir 2005 Istrien besuchten?

***Remember to buy** some milk, okay?*
Denk daran, Milch zu kaufen, ja?

Bei *forget* (vergessen), *regret* (bedauern) und *remember* (sich erinnern) hat die unterschiedliche Bedeutung mit der Zeit der Äußerung zu tun. Bezieht sich der Satz auf die **Vergangenheit,** verwenden wir die drei Verben mit der *-ing*-Form.

Handelt es sich dagegen um die **Gegenwart** oder die **Zukunft,** steht das nachfolgende Verb im Infinitiv.

stop, try, mean

*Ted must **stop smoking** or he'll be ill.*
Ted muss aufhören zu rauchen, sonst wird er krank.

*We **stopped to get** some petrol in Venlo.*
Wir hielten an, um in Venlo zu tanken.

*Why don't you **try asking** for help?*
Warum probierst du nicht mal, um Hilfe zu bitten?

*I **tried to ring** but my mobile was broken.*
Ich versuchte anzurufen, aber mein Handy war kaputt.

*If we don't go shopping, it **will mean eating** out.*
Kaufen wir nicht ein, müssen wir essen gehen.

*I **mean to speak** to Mr Davis about my mark.*
Ich bin fest dazu entschlossen, Mr Davis auf meine Note anzusprechen.

Bedeutet ***stop*** „aufhören, etwas zu tun", steht das angeschlossene Verb in der *-ing*-Form (Gerundium). Wenn ***stop*** „kurz anhalten, um etwas anderes zu tun" bedeutet, dann folgt ein Verb im Infinitiv.

Bedeutet ***try*** „ein Versuch, etwas Neues zu tun", steht das angeschlossene Verb in der *-ing*-Form (Gerundium).
Bedeutet ***try*** „ein vergeblicher Versuch, etwas zu tun", dann folgt ein Verb im Infinitiv.

Bedeutet ***mean*** „das bedeutet, dass etwas anders getan werden muss", steht das angeschlossene Verb in der *-ing*-Form (Gerundium).
Bedeutet ***mean*** „zu beabsichtigen, etwas sicherlich zu tun", dann folgt ein Verb im Infinitiv.

49

Überprüfe hier, ob das Wissen sitzt

Lies zuerst den ganzen Dialog durch. Dann setze die angegebenen Verben in der richtigen Form ein.

a **Roger** Hi, Jenny. Have you got a moment? Look, do you remember ______________________ (interview) that guy about opening an office in Germany a couple of weeks ago?

b **Jenny** Sure. His name was Alan Davis, I think. He was a pleasant man but he just couldn't stop ______________________ (talk). He's trying ______________________ (find) an agent in the Ruhrgebiet, I think.

c **Roger** Well, this email is from a guy called Joachim Stein in Essen. He'd like ______________________ (contact) Alan Davis but he says he forgot ______________________ (write down) his address and so on. I meant ______________________ (answer) it yesterday, but I just couldn't find the time. And I can't stop ______________________ (deal) with it now, I'm afraid. Do you think you could answer it for me?

d **Jenny** Sure, Roger. No problem. I'll stop ______________________ (work) on what I'm doing and answer the email immediately.

e **Roger** Thanks a lot, Jenny. I suppose it just means ______________________________ (give) Alan Davis Mr Stein's email address and then he can take it from there. I don't want ______________________________ (do) it the other way round.

f **Jenny** Of course not. We always avoid ______________________________ (pass on) somebody's address to strangers. Anyhow, luckily, I decided ______________________________ (keep) Alan Davis's contact details just in case anybody got in touch. I'll try ______________________________ (get) him on his mobile number first or I'll try ______________________________ (reach) him on his office number.

a do you remember interviewing
b he just couldn't stop talking – He's trying to find
c He'd like to contact – he forgot to write down – I meant to answer – I can't stop to deal with it
d I'll stop working
e it just means giving – I don't want to do
f We always avoid passing on – I decided to keep – I'll try to get – I'll try to reach

50

Die *-ing*-Form nach Präpositionen

Wir benutzen immer die *-ing*-Form (Gerundium) **nach Präpositionen.** Diese Regel gilt nicht nur für Präpositionen, die alleine stehen, sondern auch für **Zusammensetzungen** aus Verben/Nomen/Adjektiv + Präposition:

I joined Greenpeace ***after seeing*** *a report on TV.*
*We****'re looking forward to going*** *on holiday.*
I don't like ***the idea of changing*** *my job.*
Are you ***interested in learning*** *German?*

Überprüfe hier, ob das Wissen sitzt

1 Vervollständige die Sätze mit einer Präposition bzw. ein Partikel aus dem Kasten.

after by for in of of ~~to~~ to

a I look forward _to_ hearing from you shortly.

b Thank you ________ giving me so much of your time.

c Frank joined our club ________ seeing us play.

d Nick doesn't like the idea ________ getting a dog.

e Barbara is interested ________ applying for the job.

f You must give people an incentive ________ work hard.

g A Bloody Mary is made ________ mixing tomato juice and vodka.

h Motor racing comprises ________ driving round in circles.

2 Setze die angegebenen Verben in die richtige Form.

a In this email, they agree ____________ (pay) the bill at once.

b I wouldn't dream of ____________ (date) such a horrible man.

c We lost the game in spite of ____________ (be) one goal up for 85 minutes.

d The union has warned us not ____________ (agree) to the offer.

e In you place, I'd think about ____________ (get) expert advice.

1
a to
b for
c after
d of
e in
f to
g by
h of

2
a to pay
b dating
c being
d to agree
e getting

51

Die *-ing*-Form nach bestimmten Redewendungen

Einige **feste Redewendungen** benötigen immer die *-ing*-Form (Gerundium), z.B. *It's no good* ... (es hat keinen Zweck) und *How/What about ...?* (wie wäre es mit ...?).

It's no good asking *again. The answer's still No!*
How/What about eating *at a restaurant tonight?*

Andere Wendungen dieser Art sind:

It's no use repairing *this camera.*
It's worth seeing *that film.*
It's not worth saving *nowadays.*
Fred is stupid ***as well as being*** *lazy.*
Do something useful, ***like feeding*** *the dog.*
Can you do something to help, ***such as opening*** *the wine?*
I can't help feeling *that you are too strict with the children.*

Überprüfe hier, ob das Wissen sitzt

Trage zu jeder englischen Redewendung den Buchstaben ihrer deutschen Entsprechung ein.

It's no good asking all the time. The answer's still No!

How about eating out this evening?

It's no use having this camera repaired.

When it's worth doing, it's worth doing well.

I'm not going to waste my time listening to such nonsense.

It's not worth saving nowadays.

Do something useful, like letting the dog out, for example.

I can't help feeling that something is going wrong.

a Es hat keinen Zweck dauernd zu fragen. Die Antwort ist immer noch Nein!
b Es lohnt sich nicht, diese Kamera reparieren zu lassen.
c Heutzutage lohnt es sich nicht zu sparen.
d Ich habe nicht vor, meine Zeit zu verschwenden sich solchen Unsinn anzuhören.
e Ich werde das Gefühl nicht los, dass irgendetwas schief läuft.
f Mach was Nützliches, wie zum Beispiel den Hund rauslassen.
g Wenn schon, denn schon.
h Wie wäre es, wenn wir heute abend auswärts essen?

Die Reihenfolge der richtigen Buchstaben lautet von oben nach unten:
a
h
b
g
d
c
f
e

52

Das Partizip

Die Formen des Partizips

Das Partizip hat zwei Formen, nämlich das Partizip Präsens *(present participle)* und das Partizip Perfekt *(perfect participle)*.

*The girl **standing** over there at the bus stop is our neighbour.*
*Carr & Co is the firm **bought** by the Japanese last year.*

Das **Partizip Präsens** wird durch Anhängen von *-ing* gebildet.
Das **Partizip Perfekt** (3. Form) wird bei **regelmäßigen Verben** durch Anhängen von *-ed* gebildet; **unregelmäßige Verben** haben eine besondere Form, die man sich einfach merken muss.

Das Partizip Präsens nach Verben der Bewegung und der Ruhe

Came, ran und *goes* sind Verben der Bewegung; *sat, stood, lay* sind Verben der Ruhe. Nach solchen Verben benutzen wir das **Partizip Präsens,** um auszudrücken, dass eine zweite Handlung *(racing, shouting, fishing* usw.*)* gleichzeitig passiert.

*The car **came racing** down the road.*
*The boys **ran shouting** out of the classroom.*
*Ben **goes fishing** every weekend.*
*We **sat talking** all night.*
*Helen **stood waiting** for the bus.*
*Tom **lay reading** on his bed.*

Wir benutzen das **Partizip Präsens** auch nach dem Verb *spend* + einem Zeitausdruck *(expression of time)* im Sinne von „Zeit verbringen“:
*We **spend** hours **walking** the dog.*

Partizipien zur Verkürzung von notwendigen Relativsätzen

Ist das **Subjekt eines Relativsatzes** auch das **Subjekt des Hauptsatzes,** können wir notwendige Relativsätze mithilfe eines Partizips verkürzen.

*The woman **who is sitting** at the bar is my wife.*
*The woman **sitting** at the bar is my wife.*

*This is a firm **which is investing** in new technology.*
*This is a firm **investing** in new technology.*

*The man **that was arrested** by the police has escaped.*
*The man **arrested** by the police has escaped.*

*That is the house **that was damaged** in the storm.*
*That is the house **damaged** in the storm.*

Bei **Aktivsätzen** benutzen wir das **Partizip Präsens**, also die *-ing*-Form.
Bei **Passivsätzen** dagegen benutzen wir das **Partizip Perfekt** (3. Form).

■ **Partizipien zur Verkürzung von Adverbialsätzen**

Auch hier ist es nur dann möglich, Adverbialsätze zu verkürzen, wenn das **gleiche Subjekt** im Haupt- und Nebensatz vorkommt.

Bei **Aktivsätzen** benutzen wir die *-ing*-Form (Partizip Präsens).
***After we had got home,** we watched a video.*
***After getting home,** we watched a video.*

***Because he missed his bus,** Tom arrived late.*
***Missing his bus,** Tom arrived late.*

*I saw an accident **when I was travelling to work.***
*I saw an accident **when travelling to work.***

Bei **Passivsätzen** dagegen benutzen wir die 3. Form (Partizip Perfekt).
***When dogs are treated well,** they behave well.*
***When treated well,** dogs behave well.*

***If these two chemicals are mixed,** they explode.*
***If mixed, these two chemicals** explode.*

Diese Art Verkürzung (also das Ersetzen von Nebensätzen durch Partizipien) kommt besonders häufig in knappen Medienberichten, technischen Beschreibungen usw. vor:
*The body **which has been identified** as John Mason was found by a woman **who was taking** her dog for a walk.*
*The body **identified** as John Mason was found by a woman **taking** her dog for a walk.*

***After you have installed** the program, reboot the computer.*
***After installing** the program, reboot the computer.*

Überprüfe hier, ob das Wissen sitzt

1 Bilde Sätze mit Verben der Bewegung und der Ruhe. Einige Wörter müssen hinzugefügt werden.
he/come/storm/into/office → He came storming into the office.

a child/run/scream/upstairs

____

b Ben and Anna/often/go/dance

____

c lovers/lie/kiss/hours

____

d Julie/sit/drink/coffee

____

e crowd/stand/watch/match

____

2 Verkürze die Relativsätze mit Partizipien.
The car firm which is doing best at the moment is Italian.
The car firm doing best at the moment is Italian.

a The police officers who are stopping the traffic are helpful.

The police officers ______________________________

b The girl who is speaking now is my sister.

The girl ______________________________

c The woman who was injured in the crash has died.

The woman ______________________________

d The house that was damaged by fire must be pulled down.

The house ______________________________

3 Verkürze die Adverbialsätze mit Partizipien.

After we watched the documentary, we had a test.

After watching the documentary, we had a test.

a Because I felt ill, I missed the lesson.

____, I missed the lesson.

b I met my wife when I was working in Hamburg.

I met my wife ____.

c When modern cars are looked after properly, they last many years.

____ many years.

d If you ask those two to work together, they just play the fool.

____ the fool.

e After you have finished the letters, type this report.

____, type this report.

1 a The child ran screaming upstairs.
b Ben and Anna often go dancing.
c The lovers lay kissing for hours.
d Julie sat drinking coffee.
e The crowd stood watching the match.

2 a stopping the traffic are helpful.
b speaking now is my sister.
c injured in the crash has died.
d damaged by fire must be pulled down.

3 a Feeling ill
b when working in Hamburg
c When looked after properly, modern cars last
d If asked to work together, those two just play
e After finishing the letters

53

Der *if*-Satz

Ein ***if*-Satz** besteht aus zwei Teilen: einem ***if*-Teil** und einem **Hauptteil.** Der *if*-Teil drückt eine **Bedingung** aus, der Hauptteil eine **Folge.**

Der *if*-Teil kann vor oder nach dem Hauptteil stehen. Steht der *if*-Teil an erster Stelle, wird er von dem Hauptteil durch ein **Komma** getrennt.
If it rains, *we will stay at home.*
We will stay at home ***if it rains.***

Je nach Sinn können wir den *if*-Teil, den Hauptteil oder beide Teile eines *if*-Satzes **verneinen:**
We ***won't have*** *a picnic if it rains.*

If I ***don't get*** *the job, I will move to York.*
Wenn ich die Stelle nicht bekomme, ziehe ich nach York um.

If I get the job, I ***won't move*** *to York.*
Wenn ich die Stelle bekomme, ziehe ich nicht nach York um.

If I ***don't get*** *the job, I* ***won't move*** *to York.*
Wenn ich die Stelle nicht bekomme, ziehe ich nicht nach York um.

Bei **Fragen** können wir nur den Hauptteil als Frage bilden. Dann steht der Hauptteil an erster Stelle:
Will we have *a picnic if it rains?*

Je nach Sinn können wir **andere modale Hilfsverben** im Hauptteil verwenden.
If it doesn't rain, we ***can have*** *a picnic.*
We ***may have*** *a picnic if it doesn't rain.*
If it is dry, you ***should give*** *the plants some water.*

Die Zeitenfolge in *if*-Sätzen

Es gibt drei Typen von *if*-Sätzen, die unterschiedliche Zeitenfolgen haben:

	if-Teil	Hauptteil
Typ I	*if* + *simple present* *If you **work** hard,*	*will*-Futur / *can* / *may* / *must* *you **will pass** the test.*
Typ II	*if* + *simple past* *If you **worked** harder,*	*would* / *could* / *might* + Infinitiv *you **would pass** the test.*
Typ III	*if* + *past perfect* *If you **had worked** harder,*	*would* / *could* / *might have* + 3. Form *you **would have passed** the test.*

Weitaus die meisten Fehler werden dadurch verursacht, dass die Zeitenfolgen nicht eingehalten werden. Wichtig ist vor allem, dass *will* und *would* **nie** im *if*-Teil stehen.

Überprüfe hier, ob das Wissen sitzt

1 Verbinde einen Satzteil aus dem Kasten mit einem Satzteil unten, um sinnvolle Sätze zu bilden.

if he sees her	if it had been properly serviced	if it snows
if she had applied for it	if we all worked harder	
if you had the money	~~I'm sure she'll help you~~	
they would have won	we wouldn't have been late	

a If you ask Helen politely, *I'm sure she'll help you.*

b If the bus had come on time, ____.

c Would they pay us a bonus ____?

d Tom will give Anna your message ____.

e If they had scored one more, ____.

f We will go skiing at the weekend ____.

g Would you buy a house ____?

h The plane wouldn't have crashed ____.

i Anna would have got the job ____.

2 Vervollständige die *if*-Sätze mit den fehlenden Verbformen. Achte dabei auf die Zeitenfolge.

a If the traffic had not been so heavy, we ________________________ (arrive) earlier.

b ________________________ (Sally/do) better at school if she didn't have a part-time job?

c If the company ________________________ (modernize), it won't not grow.

d The financial system ________________________ (collapse) if we don't help the banks.

e We would not be in such difficuties if the banks ________________________ (not be) so greedy.

f If the banks did not pay big bonuses, they ________________________ (not be able to motivate) their staff.

g The government would not have saved the banks if it ________________________ (not have to protect) jobs.

h Of course the rescue package won't work if companies ________________________ (not make) use of it.

1
b we wouldn't have been late
c if we all worked harder
d if he sees her
e they would have won
f if it snows
g if you had the money
h if it had been properly serviced
i if she had applied for it

2
a would have arrived
b Would Sally do
c doesn't modernize
d will collapse
e were not
f would not be able to motivate
g had not had to protect
h don't make

54

Der Gebrauch von *if*-Sätzen

Die drei Typen von *if*-Sätzen unterscheiden sich gemäß der Wahrscheinlichkeit der zu erwartenden Folge:

Typ I Die Folge ist sicher bzw. sehr wahrscheinlich.
*If you **give** me £ 10, I **will/can/may buy** a CD.*
Wenn du mir £ 10 gibst, werde ich/kann ich eine CD kaufen/kaufe ich vielleicht eine CD.

Typ II Die Folge ist möglich, aber unwahrscheinlich.
*If you **gave me** £ 10, I **would/could/might buy** a CD.*
Wenn du mir £ 10 gäbest, würde ich/könnte ich/würde ich vielleicht eine CD kaufen.

Typ III Die Folge ist unmöglich, da wir das Ergebnis schon kennen.
*If you **had given** me £ 10, I **would/could/might have bought a** CD.*
Wenn du mir £ 10 gegeben hättest, hätte ich eine CD gekauft/hätte ich eine CD kaufen können/hätte ich vielleicht eine CD gekauft.

Die Sätze der Typen I und II beziehen sich immer nur auf die Gegenwart oder auf die Zukunft. Dies kann besonders bei Sätzen des Typs II für Verwirrung sorgen, da das Verb im *if*-Satz im *simple past* steht:
*If you **worked** harder, you **would pass** the test.*

In diesem Fall entspricht diese Zeit jedoch nicht der Vergangenheit, sondern dem deutschen Konjunktiv *(subjunctive)*:
Wenn du (jetzt) härter arbeiten würdest ...

Überprüfe hier, ob das Wissen sitzt

Vervollständige die *if*-Sätze mit den fehlenden Verbformen. Benutze den angegebenen Typ I, II oder III.

a If parents __________ (be) more sensible, they __________ __________ (not give) their children junk food. *(Typ II)*

b If healthy food __________ (not be) so expensive, maybe people __________ (buy) it. *(Typ II)*

c If internet providers __________ (cooperate), the police __________ (be able to fight) internet crime more effectively. *(Typ III)*

d __________ (you/leave) school in the summer if you __________ (manage) to find a good job with a future? *(Typ I)*

e People still at school __________ (not need) to take evening and weekend jobs if they __________ (not spend) so much of their money on clothes and electronics. *(Typ II)*

f __________ (Frank/need) to get such a low-paid job if he __________ (get) better qualifications? *(Typ III)*

g Some economists say that people in manufacturing __________ (lose) their jobs if consumers __________ (not buy) more goods than they really need. *(Typ I)*

a were – would not give
b was not – would buy
c had cooperated – would have been able to fight
d Will you leave – manage
e would not need – didn't spend
f Would Frank have needed – had got
g will lose – do not buy

Der Relativsatz

■ Relativsätze mit Relativpronomen

Ein Relativsatz ist ein **Nebensatz,** der durch ein **Relativpronomen** – *who, which, whose* – eingeleitet wird.
Wir benutzen Relativsätze, um einen Teil des Hauptsatzes durch zusätzliche Informationen genauer zu bestimmen:
This is ***the painting*** *from Spain* ***which*** *my mother bought recently.*

Für Personen benutzen wir das Relativpronomen *who* und für Dinge *which*.
The girl ***who spoke to me*** *is called Helen.*
This is the house ***which we want to buy.***

Statt *who* und *which* können wir auch *that* für Personen und Dinge einsetzen.
The boy ***that*** *won* ***the match*** *goes to our school.*
The bike ***that was stolen*** *belongs to my sister.*

■ Relativsätze mit *whose*

Um **Besitz/Zugehörigkeit** anzuzeigen, benutzen wir das Relativpronomen *whose* unmittelbar vor einem Nomen. Wir benutzen *whose* für Personen und Dinge.
Is Tom the man ***whose mother lives in the USA?***
Sally is the girl ***whose brother once played for Manchester United.***
This is the house ***whose owner died last week.***
Are these the letters ***whose addresses are wrong?***

Relativsätze ohne Relativpronomen

Ist das **Subjekt** im Hauptsatz und im Relativsatz dasselbe, benötigen wir ein Relativpronomen.

The car ***which/that caused the accident*** *is French.*

Ist dagegen das Subjekt des Hauptsatzes *(the house)* ein anderes als das Subjekt des Relativsatzes *(we)*, dann können wir das Relativpronomen weglassen.

The house ***we bought*** *is 350 years old.*

Relativsätze **ohne zwingende Relativpronomen** nennen wir *contact clauses*. Im modernen Englisch lassen wir bei solchen Sätzen das Relativpronomen möglichst weg.

Relativsätze mit Präpositionen

Kommt eine **Präposition** in einem Relativsatz vor, steht sie – genau wie bei einem Hauptsatz – normalerweise **nach dem Verb.**

Helen is the girl ***(that) I work with*** *every Saturday.*

Is this the tree Ben ***ran into*** *with his car?*

The CD ***which*** *Pat* ***was listening*** *to belongs to me.*

Was that the man who you ***were talking to*** *just now?*

Wird der Relativsatz mit *that* eingeleitet oder ohne ein Relativpronomen gebildet, muss die Präposition **nachgestellt** werden.

Bei Relativsätzen mit *which* und *who* kann die Präposition vor dem Pronomen stehen. Aus *who* wird dann *whom*. Solche Sätze wirken jedoch sehr formell.

The woman ***to whom*** *I was talking is my sister.*

Überprüfe hier, ob das Wissen sitzt

1 Welches Relativpronomen ist das richtige? Streiche die falschen durch.

a Nick and Susan King are the people who – which – whose moved into our old flat.

b The Yetti is the name of a strange being who – which – whose is said to live in these mountains.

c Claudia Fuchs was the guide who – which – whose showed us round Cologne cathedral.

d The passengers who – which – whose flight was cancelled spent the night at a hotel.

e We must rent a car who – which – whose is big enough for all our camping equpment.

f Covent Garden is a part of London who – which – whose is very popular among tourists.

g This is the field who – which – whose owners want to turn it into a car park.

2 Streiche die nicht notwendigen Relativpronomen durch, um Relativsätze ohne Relativpronomen *(contact clauses)* zu bilden.

a I am worried about the email that I received from my boss.

b The person who won the lottery gave up his job and went on a world tour.

c What did you do? The dog that bit you is normally very friendly.

d Several of the passengers who the ticket collector checked didn't have a first class ticket.

e The food that we got at the youth hostel was surprisingly good.

f The project which we're doing on climate change is quite interesting.

g The hotel also takes guests who have dogs.

3 Die Browns zeigen ihren Freunden einige Urlaubsfotos. Verbinde die Sätze mithilfe von Relativpronomen.

This is an old town in Westphalia. Its name is Soest.
This is an old town in Westphalia whose name is Soest.

a This is a part of Westphalia. It has a lot of rivers and lakes.

This is a part of Westphalia ______________________________

____

b This is a church in Münster. It is over 800 years old.

This is a church in Münster ______________________________

____

c These are our friends from Dortmund. Their names are Odile and John.

These are our friends from Dortmund ______________________________

______________________________________ Odile and John.

d And this is the palace in the Münsterland. I told you about it yesterday.

And this is the palace in the Münsterland ______________________________

______________________________________ yesterday.

1 Richtig sind: a who, d whose, g whose
b which, e which
c who, f which

2 a I am worried about the email *that* I received from my boss.
b The person who won the lottery gave up his job and went on a world tour.
c What did you do? The dog that bit you is normally very friendly.
d Several of the passengers *who* the ticket collector checked didn't have a first class ticket.
e The food *that* we got at the youth hostel was surprisingly good.
f The project *which* we're doing on climate change is quite interesting.
g The hotel also takes guests who have dogs.

3 a which has a lot of rivers and lakes
c whose names are
b which is over 800 years old
d that I told you about

56

Notwendige und nicht notwendige Relativsätze

In den ersten beiden Sätzen benötigen wir die Relativsätze, um die Sätze als Ganzes zu verstehen.
The man ***who was arrested*** *had stolen a car.*
The car ***which was stolen*** *belongs to my boss.*

Die Relativsätze machen notwendige Angaben über die Person oder die Sache, um die es im Hauptsatz geht.

Daher werden solche unentbehrlichen Relativsätze **„notwendige Relativsätze"** *(defining relative clauses)* genannt. **Notwendige Relativsätze** werden immer **ohne trennende Kommas** benutzt.

In diesen beiden Sätzen schildern die Relativsätze Nebensächlichkeiten.
*A woman****, who was out with her dog,*** *called the police.*
*This computer****, which was made in Japan,*** *works very fast.*

Lassen wir die Relativsätze weg, können wir die Hauptsätze immer noch gut verstehen.
Daher werden diese Relativsätze als **„nicht notwendig"** *(non-defining)* bezeichnet. **Nicht notwendige Relativsätze** werden immer **durch Kommas** vom Hauptsatz abgetrennt.

Überprüfe hier, ob das Wissen sitzt

Wenn es sich um einen nicht notwendigen Relativsatz handelt, setze Kommas, um den Relativsatz von dem Hauptsatz abzutrennen.

a The boy who was injured in the match had fouled another player.

b The fire which broke out last night was caused by a gas leak.

c A young man who was walking through the park saw everything that happened.

d My mobile phone which was switched off at the time had been stolen.

e The dogs we saw were all on the lead.

f The dogs which we saw in the woods were all behaving very well.

g The team that won the match has just got a new trainer.

h The Russian skaters who now live in New York were given maximum points by all the judges.

i My dad's car which he bought new only last summer has broken down yet again.

j Rod has married the girl we saw him with last June.

k The curry we had at the Shalimar was really wonderful.

l The book by Simon Beckett I am reading at the moment is incredibly exciting.

m A woman who was waiting for the bus in Oak Lane reported the two graffiti-sprayers to the police.

In diesen Sätzen sind die Relativsätze notwendig:
a, b, e, g, j, k, l.

Also mussten in diesen Sätzen Kommas gesetzt werden:

c A young man, *who was walking through the park*, saw ...

d My mobile phone, *which was switched off at the time*, had ...

f The dogs, *which we saw in the woods*, were ...

h The Russian skaters, *who now live in New York*, were given ...

i My dad's car, *which he bought new only last summer*, has ...

m A woman, *who was waiting for the bus in Oak Lane*, reported ...

57

Die indirekte Rede (Aussagen); Verschiebung der Zeiten

Wollen wir einem Dritten berichten, was während eines Gespräches gesagt oder was geschrieben wurde, benutzen wir die **indirekte Rede.** Wir benutzen dabei ein **einleitendes Verb** wie *say, tell, answer, think* usw., um zu zeigen, dass wir berichten. Die Anführungszeichen entfallen.
Tom: "I ***went*** *to the dentist's* ***yesterday.****"*
Tom ***says*** *(that)* ***he went*** *to the dentist's* ***the day before.***
Tom ***told us*** *(that)* ***he had gone*** *to the dentist's* ***the day before.***

Um das ursprüngliche Gespräch inhaltlich präzise wiederzugeben, müssen wir in der indirekten Rede einige Formulierungen ändern. Bei diesen Änderungen handelt es sich um **Zeitangaben, Ortsangaben** und natürlich um die beteiligten bzw. erwähnten **Personen.**

Steht das **einleitende Verb im Präsens,** bleiben die Zeiten des ursprünglichen Gespräches unverändert.

Steht das **einleitende Verb in der Vergangenheit,** verschieben sich die Zeiten. Handelt es sich um eine **fortbestehende Situation,** entfällt die Zeitverschiebung.
Helen: "I ***am*** *married but I* ***haven't got*** *any children."*
Helen ***answered*** *(that)* ***she is*** *married but* ***she hasn't*** *any children.*

Verschiebung der Zeiten

Direkte Rede		Indirekte Rede	
Vollverben			
simple present	*play, plays*	*simple past*	*played*
present progressive	*am/is/are playing*	*past progressive*	*was/were playing*
simple past	*played*	*past perfect*	*had played*
past progressive	*was/were playing*	*past perfect progressive*	*had been playing*

WISSEN • WISSEN • WISSEN • WISSEN • WISSEN • WISSEN

Direkte Rede		Indirekte Rede	
Vollverben			
present perfect	*has/have played*	*past perfect*	*had played*
present perfect progressive	*has/have been playing*	*past perfect progressive*	*had been playing*
past perfect	*had played*	(keine Änderung)	*had played*
will-Futur	*will play*	*would* + Infintiv	*would play*
Hilfsverben			
going to-Futur	*am/is/are going to play*	*was/were going to*	*was/were going to play*
would	*would play*	*would have* + 3. Form	*would have played*
would have	*would have played*	(keine Änderung)	*would have played*
Modale Hilfsverben			
can	*can play*	*could*	*could play*
may	*may play*	*might*	*might play*
must	*must play*	*had to*	*had to play*
should	*should play*	*should have* + 3. Form	*should have played*

Überprüfe hier, ob das Wissen sitzt

Formuliere die direkten Aussagen in die indirekte Rede um. Benutze das angegebene einleitende Verb im *simple past*.

It is September. Peter Hill and Jane Benson are telling their friends about a camping holiday they had in Scotland in August.

a Jane "We drove to Rotterdam and then we took the ferry to Hull in England." (say)

____

____

b Peter "We landed at Hull at 6 in the morning and we left for Scotland immediately." (add)

____

____

c Jane "Peter suggested spending a night in England, but I wanted to get on to Scotland." (tell + us)

____

____

d Jane "Peter finally gave way as long as I did a lot of the driving." (say with a smile)

____

____

e Peter "I found it easy to drive on the left because there was plenty of other traffic." (point out)

____

____

f Peter "Britain is quite small so we arrived at our camping site near Edinburgh in the afternoon." (tell + Ben)

____

____

g Jane "The Scots were very friendly and they gave us a warm welcome." (mention)

____

____

a Jane said that they had driven to Rotterdam and then they had taken the ferry to Hull in England.

b Peter added that they had landed at 6 in the morning and they had left for Scotland immediately.

c Jane told us that Peter had suggested spending a night in England, but she had wanted to get on to Scotland.

d Jane said with a smile that Peter had finally given way as long as she did a lot of the driving.

e Peter pointed out that he had found it easy to drive on the left because there had been plenty of other traffic.

f Peter told Ben that Britain is quite small so they had arrived at their camping site near Edinburgh in the afternoon.

g Jane mentioned that the Scots were very friendly and they had given them a warm welcome.

58

Die indirekte Rede: Verschiebung der Zeit-, Orts- und Personenangaben

Ähnlich wie im Deutschen ändern sich die **Zeitangaben** und **Ortsangaben** nur, wenn sie sich bis zum Zeitpunkt der Wiedergabe (indirekten Rede) auch verändert haben.
"I met him today."
She said she had met him ***today.*** (am gleichen Tag)
She said she had met him ***on that day.*** (an einem folgenden Tag)

Direkte Rede	Indirekte Rede
today	*on that day*
tomorrow	*the next day*
yesterday	*the day before*
the day after tomorrow	*two days later*
the day before yesterday	*two days before*
last week/month/...	*the week/month/... before*
next week/month/...	*the following week/month/...*
two/... days/weeks/... ago	*two/... days/weeks/... before*
now	*then*
at the moment	*at that moment*
here	*there*
this/these	*that/those*

Verschiebung bei Personen

Pronomen müssen ebenfalls oft durch Nomen oder andere Pronomen ersetzt werden, damit der Inhalt verständlich ist:

*Tom: "**I** am going home now."*
*Tom said **he** was going home then.*

*Helen: "**I** have just telephoned **him.**"*
*Helen said **she** had just telephoned **Ben Snow.***

*Helen/Tom: "**We** are playing cards tonight."*
*Helen and Tom said **they** were playing cards that night.*

*Helen: "**I'm** doing **it** now, **Tom.**"*
*Helen told **Tom she** was doing **the report** then.*

Überprüfe hier, ob das Wissen sitzt

1 Ergänze die fehlenden Formulierungen in der Tabelle.

Direkte Rede	Indirekte Rede
today	on that day
	the next day
yesterday	
the day after tomorrow	
	two days before
last week/month/...	
	the following week/month/...
two/... days/weeks/... ago	
now	
	at that moment
here	
	that/those

2 Welche Pronomen müssen hier eingesetzt werden?

a Tom: "**I** am going home now."

Tom said _______ was going home then.

b Helen: "**I** have just telephoned ________________."

Helen said ________________ had just telephoned **Ben Snow.**

c Helen/Tom: "**We** are playing cards tonight."

Helen and Tom said _______________ were playing cards that night.

d Helen: "**I**'m doing ____________ now, **Tom.**"

Helen told **Tom** _______________ was doing **the report** then.

1 Vergleiche deine Lösung mit der Tabelle auf Seite 168.

2 a he

b him – she

c they

d it – she

59

Die indirekte Rede: Fragen, Bitten und Aufforderungen

Fragen mit und ohne Fragewort

Bei **indirekten Fragen** unterscheiden wir zwischen **Fragen mit Fragewort** *(how?, what?, where?* usw.*)* und **Fragen ohne Fragewort.**

*Helen: "**Where** is Tom?"*
*Helen asked **where** Tom was.*

*Tom: "**How much** did the wine cost?"*
*Tom wanted to know **how much** the wine had cost.*

*Ben: "**Have you worked** here long, Helen?"*
*Ben asked Helen **if/whether** she had worked there long.*

Bei **Fragen mit Fragewort** wird das Fragewort einfach übernommen. Das Subjekt steht dann wie bei Aussagen vor dem Verb und das Fragezeichen entfällt.

Die Tatsache, dass es sich um eine Frage handelt, wird durch das **einleitende Verb** *(asked, wanted to know)* und das **Fragewort** *(where?, how much?)* ausgedrückt.

Bei **Fragen ohne Fragewort** benutzen wir *if* bzw. *whether* (ob), um zu verdeutlichen, dass es sich um eine Frage handelt.

*Ann: "**Do you often go** to the cinema, Tom?"*
*Ann asked Tom **if/whether** he often went to the cinema.*

Wie bei Aussagen müssen oft die **Zeitform des Verbs, Zeitangaben, Ortsangaben** und die **Personen** geändert werden.

Bitten und Aufforderungen

Indirekte Bitten und **Aufforderungen** werden stets durch *asked* (bitten) bzw. *told* in der Bedeutung von „sagen“ eingeleitet.

*Helen: “Tom, **help** me with the shopping, please.”*
*Helen **asked** Tom **to help** her with the shopping.*

*Tom: “**Deliver** the books tomorrow.”*
*Tom **told** the shop **to deliver** the books the next day.*

*Ben: “**Don’t forget** to phone the airport, Ann.”*
*Ben told Ann **not to forget** to phone the airport.*

Beachte: Die Verben *ask* und *tell* haben immer ein **Objekt,** daher muss die angesprochene Person erwähnt werden.

Das **Verb des indirekten Aufforderungssatzes** erscheint als *to*-Infinitiv.

Bei **verneinten indirekten Aufforderungen** setzen wir *not* unmittelbar vor *to.*

Überprüfe hier, ob das Wissen sitzt

1 Formuliere die direkten Fragen in indirekte Fragen um. Achte auf den Unterschied zwischen Fragen mit und ohne Fragewort.

Some reporters are asking Frank Banks, a police officer, about a bank robbery.

a When did the robbery take place? (ask + police officer)

John Morse ____

____

b Was anybody hurt during the robbery? (want to know)

Alison Fox ____

____

c What can you tell us about the method of entry? (enquire)

Sarah Medway ____

______________________________ about the method of entry.

d Do you have any information about how much money was stolen? (wonder)

Alison ______________________________ any information about

____

e How many people were in the bank at the time? (ask)

John ____

______________________________ in the bank at the time.

f Is the bank equipped with security cameras? (enquire)

A reporter ____

______________________________ with security cameras.

2 Sally Gibbs, a crime prevention officer, is telling some motorists how to prevent car crime. Benutze das angegebene einleitende Verb.

a Always lock the car and the steering wheel. (tell + us)

Sally Gibbs ____

______________________________ the car and the steering wheel.

b Don't hide valuables like cameras under the seats. (ask + the motorists)

The officer ____

______________________________________ valuables in their cars.

c Always try to park in a supervised car park. (advise + her listeners)

She ____

__________________________ ________ in a supervised car park.

d Don't leave car documents in the car, but take them with you. (tell + us)

Officer Gibbs ______________________ car documents in the car,

but ____

1 a John Morse asked the police officer when the robbery had taken place.
b Alison Fox wanted to know if anybody had been hurt during the robbery.
c Sarah Medway enquired what Frank Banks could tell them about the method of entry.
d Alison wondered if he had any information about how much money had been stolen.
e John asked how many people had been in the bank at the time.
f A reporter enquired if the bank is equipped with security cameras.

2 a Sally Gibbs told us to always lock the car and the steering wheel.
b The officer asked the motorists not to hide valuables in their cars.
c She advised her listeners to always try to park in a supervised car park.
d Officer Gibbs told us not to leave car documents in the car, but to take them with us.

60

Bejahte und verneinte Aussagen

Wortstellung in bejahten Aussagen

	Subjekt	Prädikat	Objekt	andere Teile
1	*We*	*live*		*in Bochum.*
2	*Tom*	*watches*	*TV*	*every day.*
3	*Helen*	*made*	*breakfast*	*today.*

Die Wortstellung in Aussagen ist streng festgelegt: **Subjekt – Prädikat – andere Satzteile** (siehe Satz 1).
Gibt es im Satz ein **Objekt,** steht es unmittelbar und unzertrennlich **nach dem Prädikat** (siehe Sätze 2 und 3).

Anders als im Deutschen bleibt im Englischen die Wortstellung immer erhalten, auch wenn andere Satzteile vorangestellt werden.
Zum Vergleich:
We visited my brother in London.
Wir haben meinen Bruder in London besucht.

Yesterday we visited my brother in London.
Gestern haben wir meinen Bruder in London besucht.

Wortstellung in Aussagen mit zwei Objekten

	Subjekt	Prädikat	Objekte (wem?)	(wen/was?)	andere Teile
1	*Tom*	*sent*	***me***	***an email***	*today.*
2	*Helen*	*gave*	***Tom***	***a kiss***	*just now.*

Einige Verben – wie *send, give, promise* (versprechen) und *present* (überreichen) – haben zwei Objekte, das **indirekte Objekt** (wem?) und das **direkte Objekt** (wen? oder was?).
In Sätzen mit zwei Objekten steht das indirekte Objekt (wem?) vor dem direkten Objekt (wen? oder was?) (siehe Sätze 1 und 2).

Wortstellung in verneinten Aussagen

	Subjekt	Hilfsverb + *not/n't*	Vollverb	Objekt	andere Teile
1	*You*	***must not***	***drive***		*so fast here.*
2	*We*	***haven't***	***seen***	*this film*	*before.*
3	*I*	***don't***	***like***	*fish*	*much.*
4	*Helen*	***doesn't***	***visit***	*her parents*	*very often.*
5	*They*	***didn't***	***have***	*a holiday*	*last year.*

Wollen wir eine Aussage **verneinen,** stellen wir *not* **unmittelbar hinter das Hilfsverb** (wie in Satz 1).

In der **gesprochenen Sprache** hängen wir die Kurzform von *not* – *n't* – direkt an das Hilfsverb (siehe Satz 2).

Kommt **kein Hilfsverb** vor, benutzen wir als Ersatz *(substitute)* die Verneinung von *do:*
do not/don't (wie in Satz 3)
does not/doesn't (wie in Satz 4)
did not/didn't (wie in Satz 5)

Überprüfe hier, ob das Wissen sitzt

1 Trage die Wörter und Ausdrücke unten richtig in die Tabelle ein. Achte auf die richtige Wortstellung und Großschreibung am Satzanfang.

Nr.	Subjekt	Verbteil	indirektes Objekt	direktes Objekt	andere Teile
a					.
b					.
c	*Ben*				.
d					.
e					.
f					.

a in front of the car / didn't run / the dog

b on TV / enjoy / we / a good film

c Ann / Ben / as he left / a kiss / gave

d in Rotterdam / the truck / a ferry / went on

e a lot / the company / on computers / has spent

f to keep fit / the team / the trainer / promised

2 Bringe zuerst die Wörter der Nebensätze in die richtige Reihenfolge, indem du die Wörter in den Klammern nummerierst. Dann trage den Buchstaben des Hauptsatzes im Kästchen ein, der sinnvoll zu dem Nebensatz passt.

a We enjoy going for a bike ride ...

b The dog often sleeps on the sofa ...

c I don't like playing cards with Ben ...

d Sarah told Jack to take his shoes off ...

e Some people put on a lot of weight ...

f We had to stay at a hotel ...

g Of course the firm will go bankrupt ...

h Of course you are not hungry ...

... smoking [ ] they [ ] after [ ] give up [ ].

... just [ ] because [ ] can't lose [ ] he [ ].

... our key with us [ ] neither of us [ ] had [ ] because [ ].

... are not [ ] when [ ] at home [ ] we [ ].

... you [ ] between meals [ ] when [ ] so much [ ] eat [ ].

... were covered [ ] because [ ] with mud [ ] they [ ].

... is [ ] good [ ] if [ ] the weather [ ].

... can't sell [ ] they [ ] their products [ ] if [ ].

1 a The dog didn't run in front of the car.
b We enjoy a good film on TV.
c Ben gave Ann a kiss as he left.
d The truck went on a ferry in Rotterdam.
e The company has spent a lot on computers.
f The team promised the trainer to keep fit.

2 e + ... after they give up smoking.
c + ... because he just can't lose.
f + ... because neither of us had our key with us.
b + ... when we are not at home.
h + ... when you eat so much between meals.
d + ... because they were covered with mud.
a + ... if the weather is good.
g + ... if they can't sell their products.

61

Bejahte und verneinte Aufforderungen

Bejahte Aufforderungen haben dieselbe Form wie der Infinitiv (ohne *to*). Diese Form von Aufforderungen heißt in der Grammatik auch „Imperativ".

***Drive** carefully. The roads are wet.*

***Sit down,** please, Mr Snow.*

Verneinte Aufforderungen bilden wir mit *do not/don't* + Infinitiv (ohne *to*).

***Do not forget** to bring your books tomorrow.*

***Don't be** angry, Tom.*

Verneinte Aufforderungen mit *do not* wirken formell und streng. Daher benutzen wir normalerweise die **Kurzform** *don't*.

Möchten wir einen **Vorschlag** in Form einer Aufforderung machen, benutzen wir *let's* + Infinitiv (ohne *to*) bzw. *let's not* + Infinitiv (ohne *to*).

*I know. **Let's go** to the cinema tonight.*

***Let's not invite** that awful Harry to our party.*

Normalerweise verwenden wir im Englischen **kein Ausrufezeichen** *(exclamation mark)* nach Aufforderungssätzen:

Hurry up. And don't be so bad-tempered.

Beeil dich! Und sei nicht so griesgrämig!

Überprüfe hier, ob das Wissen sitzt

Bilde Sätze mit der Befehlsform. Einige Wörter müssen hinzugefügt werden. Achte auf Pluralformen.

a Doctor: put out/your/tongue → Put out your tongue, please.

b Teacher: not forget/bring/workbook/next lesson ______________________

____

____, please.

c Police officer: get out/your car/and/show/car papers ______________

____

____, please.

d Referee: not shout /me/like that

____, please.

b Don't forget to bring your workbooks to the next lesson
c Get out of your car and show me your car papers
d Don't shout at me like that

Entscheidungsfragen und Kurzantworten

Entscheidungsfragen

Is *this your car, madam?*
Have *you read this book?*
Can *you speak German, Ben?*
Do *you know Ben's wife?*
Does *Helen work in London?*
Did *you see the film on TV yesterday?*

Diese Fragen sind alle **Entscheidungsfragen,** die eine Antwort mit *Yes* bzw. *No* erwarten. Anders als im Deutschen können wir im Englischen solche Fragen nur mit einem Hilfsverb bilden.

Ist ein Hilfsverb schon vorhanden, benutzen wir es, um die Frage zu bilden: *is, have, can.*

Gibt es kein Hilfsverb im Satz, dann müssen wir *do* (Präsens), *does* (3. Person Singular Präsens) oder *did* (Vergangenheit) benutzen.

Im Englischen benutzen wir *be* immer so, als ob es ein Hilfsverb wäre, sogar dann, wenn kein anderes Vollverb im Satz vorhanden ist .
Are *they all at home, dear?*

Kurzantworten

Frage	Bejaht	Verneint
Can *you ride a bike?*	*Yes, I* ***can.***	*No,* ***I can't.***
Are *Ann and Ben on holiday?*	*Yes, they* ***are.***	*No, they* ***aren't.***
Have *you seen Helen?*	*Yes, I* ***have.***	*No, I* ***haven't.***
Do *you like dogs?*	*Yes, I* ***do.***	*No, I* ***don't.***
Does *Helen work in London?*	*Yes, she* ***does.***	*No, she* ***doesn't.***
Did *you watch TV last night?*	*Yes, I* ***did.***	*No, I* ***didn't.***

Da eine einfache *Yes/No-answer* etwas schroff wirken kann, benutzen wir im Englischen **Kurzantworten,** um eine Antwort auf eine Entscheidungsfrage freundlicher klingen zu lassen.

Die Form von Kurzantworten wird durch den Hauptsatz bestimmt. Das dort vorhandene **Hilfsverb** wird nochmals benutzt, um die Kurzantwort zu bilden.

Das Subjekt des Fragesatzes tritt in Form eines **Personalpronomens** auch als Subjekt der Kurzantwort auf.

Ist die Frage mit *Is/Are there* (= Gibt es?) eingeleitet, bilden wir die Kurzantwort ebenfalls mit *there:*
Is there *a car park near here?*
Yes, ***there is.*** */ No,* ***there isn't.***

Überprüfe hier, ob das Wissen sitzt

1 Bilde Fragen mit *do/does/did.* Einige Wörter müssen hinzugefügt werden.

a Tom Carr + work/here/please/?

____

b you + watch /thriller/TV/Sunday/?

____

c Mrs Coe + go/supermarket/every day/?

____

d the skaters + train/Mondays/?

____

e I + understand/you/just now/?

____

f your class + enjoy/learn/English/?

____

g Ben + take/Bonzo/walk/before/leave/work/this morning/?

____

h Sarah + usually drive/work/or/she + catch/bus/?

____

2 Füge Kurzantworten hinzu. Achte auf Pronomen.

a Do you live in Germany?

Yes, I do. No, I don't.

b Have you ever been to the USA?

____

c Is your name Julia Harris?

____

d Did Ben have a holiday last year?

____

e Are Ben and Anna married?

____

f Can Julia speak French?

____

g Did the boys have to go to hospital?

____

h Has the boss gone home yet?

____

1
a Please, does Tom Carr work here?
b Did you watch the thriller on TV on Sunday?
c Does Mrs Coe go to the supermarket every day?
d Do the skaters train on Mondays?
e Did I understand you just now?
f Does your class enjoy learning English?
g Did Ben take Bonzo for a walk before he left for work this morning?
h Does Sarah usually drive to work or does she catch a bus?

2
b Yes, I have. No, I haven't.
c Yes, it is. No, it isn't.
d Yes, he did. No, he didn't.
e Yes, they are. No, they aren't.
f Yes, she can. No, she can't.
g Yes, they did. No, they didn't.
h Yes, he has. No, he hasn't.

63

Fragen mit Fragewörtern und Frageanhängsel

Fragen mit Fragewörtern

Fragen mit **einleitendem Fragewort** bilden wir genau wie andere Fragen. Das Fragewort wird dabei vorangestellt.

How do you turn *on the TV?*
When do we have *Biology today?*
Where can I buy *some stamps?*
Why is he hitting *the dog again?*

Bei **Fragen mit *what?* und *who?*** verfahren wir anders.
Ist *what?* bzw. *who?* das Subjekt des Satzes, dann benötigen wir **kein Hilfsverb,** um Fragen zu bilden:

What happened *when you opened the box?*
Who teaches *you English?*

Ist aber das Fragewort das **Objekt** des Satzes, dann bilden wir Fragen **mit einem Hilfsverb,** also wie gewöhnlich:

What does *this word* ***mean*** *in English?*
Who do you like *best, Tom or Ben?*

Weitere Hinweise zum Gebrauch von *what?, which?, who?*

Mit *what* fragen wir nach Dingen aus einer **unbeschränkten Zahl** und mit *which* nach Dingen aus einer **beschränkten Zahl.**

What *are your hobbies?*
Which *do you like best, football or basketball?*

Mit *who* fragen wir nach **Personen** aus einer unbeschränkten sowie einer beschränkten Zahl.

Who *were you talking to on the phone?*
Who *do you think will win the race, Jane or Maureen?*

Vor ***of*-Fügungen** steht *which* für Personen und für Dinge:

Which of *the boys saw the accident?*
Which of *the CDs do you like best?*

Frageanhängsel

Die englischen *question tags* wie *isn't it?, can't you?* und *was he?* entsprechen den deutschen Frageanhängseln „nicht?"/„nicht wahr?", „oder?"/ „oder nicht?" usw.

*Cardiff **is** in Wales, **isn't** it?*
*You **can** swim, **can't** you?*
*Tom **wasn't** in his office, **was** he?*

Gibt es ein **Hilfsverb** im Satz, benutzen wir dieses, um das *question tag* zu bilden.

*You **haven't** always lived here, **have** you?*
*You **don't** know Ben's wife Ann, **do** you?*
*They **didn't** come to the party, **did** they?*

Falls **kein Hilfsverb** vorhanden ist, verwenden wir *do/does/did,* genau wie bei der Fragebildung.

*The Japanese **drive** on the left, **don't** they?*
*Helen **went** home early yesterday, **didn't** she?*

Ist das **Verb im Hauptsatz** bejaht (+), dann ist das *question tag* verneint (–) und umgekehrt.

+	–
*Cardiff **is** in Wales,*	***isn't** it?*
–	+
*Tom **wasn't** at home,*	***was** he?*

TESTEN • TESTEN • TESTEN • TESTEN • TESTEN • TESTEN • TESTEN

Überprüfe hier, ob das Wissen sitzt

1 Stelle Fragen mit Fragewörtern zu den markierten Satzteilen. Achte auf Pronomen.

Ben and Anna have just bought a flat in Cherry Lane.
→ Where have Ben and Anna bought a flat?
Anna didn't come to my party because she was in France.
→ Why didn't Anna come to your party?

a You programme the DVD recorder by pressing this button.

____

______________________________________ the DVD recorder?

b There were ten cars ahead of me in the queue.

____

______________________________________ in the queue?

c Alison has been waiting to see the dentist for over an hour.

____

______________________________________ the dentist?

d Our ferry leaves Calais at 6 o'clock on Tuesday.

____

______________________________________ Calais?

e Helen found a good job in Cologne.

____

______________________________________ a good job?

f Ben couldn't take Bonzo out because he had to go to work.

____

____

2 Vervollständige die Fragen mit *what?*, *which*? oder *who?* wie im Beispiel

Which of these books belongs to you?

a ______________________ is your name, please?

b ______________________ did you meet at the café?

c ______________________ stocks *(führen)* Swiss shoes here?

d ______________________ of the two men damaged my car?

e ______________________ happens if you press this button?

f ______________________ TV programme do you like best?

3 Bilde die fehlenden Frageanhängseln.

a The Greens haven't got any children, ______________________

b There are 32 pupils in your class, ______________________

c You met those people on holiday, ______________________

d That girl over there is your sister, ______________________

e Chris will be at the meeting on Friday, ______________________

f Don't complain to me. I can't do anything about it, ______________________

g You don't know where my keys are, ______________________

h Ben doesn't speak German, ______________________

1 a How do you proramme
b How many cars were ahead of you
c How long has Alison been waiting to see
d When does our ferry leave
e Where did Helen find
f Why couldn't Ben take Bonzo out?

2 a What
b Who
c Who
d Which
e What
f Which

3 Immer mit Komma anhängen:
a have they?
b aren't there?
c didn't you?
d isn't she?
e won't he?
f can I?
g do you?
h does he?

ANHANG

Die folgenden Wendungen weichen vom deutschen Gebrauch stark ab. Sie sind daher besonders „fehlerträchtig“.

Präpositionen der Zeit

at Christmas	zu Weihnachten
at 18 (years of age)	mit 18
at *6 o'clock*	um 6 Uhr
at mealtimes	bei Mahlzeiten
at lunch time	in der Mittagszeit
at breakfast/...	beim Frühstück/...
at the/this/that time	zu der/dieser/jener Zeit
at all times	jederzeit
at night	bei Nacht
at the weekend/at weekends	am Wochenende
at the moment	im Moment
at once	sofort
at one time	früher
at present	zur Zeit
at times	gelegentlich
in time	rechtzeitig
in the morning/evening/...	am Morgen/Abend/...
in a minute/moment	gleich
in no time	sekundenschnell
on time	planmäßig
on the hour	zur vollen Stunde

Beachte: *last* und *next* werden ohne eine Präposition benutzt:
I saw Jane ***last Friday.***
We are going to Austria ***next winter.***

Präpositionen des Ortes

at the station	am Bahnhof
at the baker's	beim Bäcker
at the chemist's	in der Apotheke
at the supermarket	im Supermarkt
at my parents' (home)	bei meinen Eltern
at the door	an der Haustür
at 20 Church Street	in der Church Street 20
at work	bei der Arbeit
at the seaside	am Meer
at a meeting	bei einer Sitzung
at a concert	in einem Konzert
at Jill's party	auf Jills Party
at the table	am Tisch
in the street	auf der Straße
in the sky	am Himmel
in the country	auf dem Land
in the picture/photo	auf dem Bild/Foto
in the foreground/background	im Vorder-/Hintergrund
in the container	in dem Behälter
in the world	auf der Welt
on the road	auf der Straße
on the board	an der Tafel
on the wall	an der Wand
on the beach	am Strand
on the coast	an der Küste
on the Rhine/Main/...	am Rhein/Main/...
on the Ruhr/Danube/...	an der Ruhr/Donau/...
on the bus/plane/...	im Bus/Flugzeug/...
on the first/... floor	im ersten/... Stock
on the way to	unterwegs nach
on the left/right	links/rechts

Andere Präpositionen

at $4,50	für $4,50
at last	endlich
at least	mindestens
not at all	überhaupt nicht
at any rate	zumindest
at first sight	auf den ersten Blick
in your own words	mit eigenen Worten
in other words	mit anderen Worten
in a loud/quiet voice	mit lauter/leiser Stimme
in my opinion/view	meiner Meinung nach
in love with	verliebt in
in German/English/...	auf Deutsch/Englisch/...
in the end	schließlich
in addition to	zusätzlich zu
in any case	auf jeden Fall
in comparison	im Vergleich
in conclusion	zum Schluss
in a hurry	in Eile
in different ways	auf verschiedene Weise
in ink/ballpoint	mit Tinte/dem Kugelschreiber
on the radio/TV	im Radio/Fernsehen
on the phone	am Telefon
on holiday	im Urlaub
on foot	zu Fuß
on occasion	gelegentlich
by bus/bike/car/...	mit dem Bus/Rad/Auto/...
by Mozart/Bach/...	von Mozart/Bach/...
on business	geschäftlich unterwegs
on display	ausgestellt (z.B. im Fenster)

Geläufige *phrasal verbs*

Oft ist es nicht möglich, die Bedeutung eines *phrasal verb* von den einzelnen Wörtern her zu erschließen. Deshalb ist es wichtig, *phrasal verbs* als Ganzes auswendig zu lernen.

My car ***broke down*** *on the way home.* (eine Panne haben)
Why should women ***bring up*** *children alone?* (erziehen)
Why don't you ***call in*** *when you're in London?* (vorbeischauen)
Stop shouting. ***Calm down*** *and we'll talk about it.* (sich beruhigen)
I'm afraid we can't ***carry out*** *the repairs until next week.* (durchführen)

We must ***check in*** *by six o'clock.* (sich abfertigen lassen)
Please ***clear away*** *your things now.* (wegräumen)
Can you help me to ***clear up*** *the kitchen, please?* (aufräumen)
Hello, Mr Snow. ***Come in,*** *please.* (hereinkommen)
Poor Mrs Coe ***fell over*** *and hurt her knee.* (hin-/umfallen)

Did you ***find out*** *anything about the accident?* (herausfinden)
Don't ***get off*** *the train before it stops.* (aussteigen)
Get on *the bus in Park Road.* (einsteigen)
Do you always ***get up*** *at 6?* (aufstehen)
When there's a fight, Bonzo never ***gives in.*** (nachgeben)

You should ***give up*** *smoking.* (aufgeben)
Go on. *What happened then?* (weitermachen)
Is Mary really ***going out*** *with that horrible man?* (ausgehen)
The thief ***got away*** *in a stolen car.* (entkommen)
Did your mother ***grow up*** *in Hamburg?* (aufwachsen)

Don't ***leave out*** *any questions. Answer them all.* (auslassen)
Why should I always ***look after*** *the dog?* (sich kümmern um)
Have you seen Bob? I've ***looked for*** *him everywhere.* (suchen)
We're really ***looking forward to*** *our holiday.* (sich freuen auf)
Look out! *The lights are red!* (aufpassen)

Anhang

***Look up** the words in your dictionary.* (nachschlagen)
*You can **pick up** the parcel at the post office.* (abholen)
*You can **put away** your books now.* (wegräumen)
***Put on** a pullover. It's cold outside.* (anziehen)
*We must **set off** early tomorrow.* (aufbrechen)

*Everybody **stood up** to see what was happening.* (aufstehen)
*We **stayed up** until 3 am yesterday.* (aufbleiben)
Take off** your coat and **sit down. (Kleidung ausziehen; sich hinsetzen)
*Always **try on** shoes before buying them.* (anprobieren)
***Turn down** the TV, please. I'm on the phone.* (leiser stellen)

*You **turn off** the computer here, okay?* (ausschalten)
***Turn up** the radio, please. I want to hear the news.* (lauter stellen)
*Keep quiet. You'll **wake up** the baby.* (aufwecken)
*I didn't **wake up** until 10 on Sunday.* (aufwachen)
*Mum was **washing up** when I got home.* (spülen)

*Jane can **work out** 234.89 × 6.7 in her head.* (ausrechnen)
*I hope you **wrote down** Monika's email address this time.* (aufschreiben)

Geläufige *prepositional verbs*

*Carr & Company is **advertising for** more workers.* (werben für)
*He **advised against** buying such an expensive car.* (raten gegen)
*We **arrived at** the station late.* (ankommen)
*The old man **asked for** some food.* (bitten um)
*Most people don't **believe in** paradise.* (glauben an)

*The cat **belongs to** our neighbour.* (gehören)
*Tom **borrowed** that CD **from** my brother.* (ausleihen von)
*We were **criticized for** being late.* (kritisieren wegen)
*Please **divide into** four groups.* (unterteilen in)
*Don't **dream about** winning the lottery. Get a job.* (träumen von)

*She **got over** her illness very quickly.* (erholen von)
*Do you **know about** the accident?* (wissen von)
*You shouldn't **laugh at** other people.* (auslachen)
*Jane **lent** this book **to** me.* (leihen)
*We **listened to** music all evening.* (zuhoren)

***Look at** that notice. It says 'Danger'.* (anschauen)
*I **read about** the match in the paper.* (lesen über)
*We **succeeded in** winning the match.* (gelingen)
*I'll **wait for** you at the station.* (warten auf)
*Most people **wish for** good health above all else.* (wünschen sich)

*Our team **won by** three goals.* (gewinnen mit)
*I often **wonder about** Sarah's behaviour.* (sich wundern über)
*I must **write to** my grandmother today.* (schreiben an)

Anhang

Unregelmäßige Verben

be	*was/were*	*been*	sein
beat	*beat*	*beaten*	schlagen, besiegen
become	*became*	*become*	werden
begin	*began*	*begun*	anfangen
blow	*blew*	*blown*	blasen, wehen
break	*broke*	*broken*	(zer)brechen
bring	*brought*	*brought*	bringen
build	*built*	*built*	bauen
buy	*bought*	*bought*	kaufen
catch	*caught*	*caught*	fangen
choose	*chose*	*chosen*	auswählen, aussuchen
come	*came*	*come*	kommen
cost	*cost*	*cost*	kosten
cut	*cut*	*cut*	schneiden
do	*did*	*done*	tun, machen, erledigen
draw	*drew*	*drawn*	zeichnen
dream	*dreamt*	*dreamt*	träumen
drink	*drank*	*drunk*	trinken, saufen
drive	*drove*	*driven*	fahren, (an)treiben
eat	*ate*	*eaten*	essen, fressen
fall	*fell*	*fallen*	(hin)fallen
feed	*fed*	*fed*	füttern

feel	*felt*	*felt*	sich fühlen
fight	*fought*	*fought*	(be)kämpfen
find	*found*	*found*	finden
fly	*flew*	*flown*	fliegen
forget	*forgot*	*forgotten*	vergessen
freeze	*froze*	*frozen*	(ge)frieren
get	*got*	*got*	bekommen, erhalten
give	*gave*	*given*	geben, schenken
go	*went*	*gone*	gehen
grow	*grew*	*grown*	wachsen, zunehmen
hang	*hung*	*hung*	(auf)hängen
have	*had*	*had*	haben, besitzen
hear	*heard*	*heard*	hören
hide	*hid*	*hidden*	verstecken
hit	*hit*	*hit*	schlagen, aufprallen
hold	*held*	*held*	(fest)halten
hurt	*hurt*	*hurt*	verletzen
keep	*kept*	*kept*	behalten, wiederholt tun
know	*knew*	*known*	kennen, wissen
lay	*laid*	*laid*	(ver)legen, hinstellen
lead	*led*	*led*	führen, leiten
lean	*leant*	*leant*	(sich) lehnen, stützen
learn	*learnt*	*learnt*	lernen, aneignen

leave	*left*	*left*	verlassen
lend	*lent*	*lent*	(ver-/aus)leihen
let	*let*	*let*	lassen
lie	*lay*	*lain*	liegen
light	*lit*	*lit*	anzünden
lose	*lost*	*lost*	verlieren
make	*made*	*made*	machen
mean	*meant*	*meant*	bedeuten
meet	*met*	*met*	sich treffen
pay	*paid*	*paid*	(be)zahlen
put	*put*	*put*	serten, stellen, legen
read	*read*	*read*	lesen
ride	*rode*	*ridden*	reiten, Rad fahren
ring	*rang*	*rung*	läuten, klingeln, anrufen
rise	*rose*	*risen*	steigen, zunehmen
run	*ran*	*run*	laufen, rennen
say	*said*	*said*	sagen
see	*saw*	*seen*	sehen, verstehen
sell	*sold*	*sold*	verkaufen
send	*sent*	*sent*	senden, schicken
shake	*shook*	*shaken*	schütteln
shoot	*shot*	*shot*	(er)schießen
show	*showed*	*shown*	zeigen

shut	*shut*	*shut*	schließen
sing	*sang*	*sung*	singen
sit	*sat*	*sat*	sitzen
sleep	*slept*	*slept*	schlafen
smell	*smelt*	*smelt*	riechen, duften
speak	*spoke*	*spoken*	sprechen
spend	*spent*	*spent*	ausgeben, verbringen
stand	*stood*	*stood*	stehen
steal	*stolen*	*stolen*	stehlen
strike	*struck*	*struck*	schlagen
swim	*swam*	*swum*	schwimmen
take	*took*	*taken*	nehmen
teach	*taught*	*taught*	unterrichten, lehren
tear	*tore*	*torn*	(zer)reißen
tell	*told*	*told*	erzählen, mitteilen, sagen
think	*thought*	*thought*	denken, meinen
throw	*threw*	*thrown*	werfen
understand	*understood*	*understood*	verstehen
wake	*woke*	*woken*	wecken
wear	*wore*	*worn*	tragen, anhaben
win	*won*	*won*	gewinnen
write	*wrote*	*written*	schreiben

Englische Wendungen

bark up the wrong tree – auf dem Holzweg sein
be a flash in the pan – ein Strohfeuer sein
be against the odds – unwahrscheinlich sein
be all the rage – der letzte Schrei sein
be a pain in the neck/arse – jdm. auf die Nerven gehen
be a sight for sore eyes – eine Augenweide sein
be between a rock and a hard place – in einer Zwickmühle sein
be dead beat – erschöpft sein
be fed up with sb./sth. – von etwas/jdm. die Nase voll haben
be hand in glove with sb. – mit jdm. unter einer Decke stecken
be left holding the baby – mit der Verantwortung alleingelassen sein
be off the record – nicht für die Öffentlichkeit sein
be on the make – sich die eigenen Taschen füllen
be on the rocks – am Ende sein
be on the safe side – ganz sicher gehen
be on the waggon – das Alkoholtrinken aufgegeben haben
be out of one's depth – überfordert sein
be right up one's street – genau nach dem Geschmack von jdm. sein
be sitting pretty – gut dran sein
be too big for one's boots – größenwahnsinnig sein
be unable to get a word in edgeways/edgewise – überhaupt nicht zu Wort kommen
be upfront with sb. – mit jdm. offen und ehrlich sein
be up the creek without a paddle – in der Klemme sein
bite off more than one can chew – sich zuviel zumuten

catch sb. doing sth. red-handed – jdn. auf frischer Tat erwischen
come in handy for sth. – für etwas nützlich sein
come to the point – zur Sache kommen
cut down on sth. – etwas einschränken

do sb. a good turn – jdm. einen Gefallen tun
do sth. for kicks – etwas aus Vergnügen tun
do sth. just for laughs – etwas zum Spaß machen

eat one's words – eine Äußerung kleinlaut zurücknehmen

fall into line with sb./sth. – mit etwas/jdm. einverstanden sein
find sth. out by trial and error – etwas durch Versuch und Irrtum herausfinden
fly off the handle – ausrasten

get a piece/slice of the action – am geschäftlichen Erfolg teilnehmen
get away with sth. – ungestraft davonkommen
get (hold of) the wrong end of the stick – etwas völlig falsch verstehen
get one's act together – etwas besser regeln/„gebacken kriegen"
get on sb.'s nerves – jdm. auf die Nerven gehen
get real – *realistisch werden*
get up sb.'s/one's nose – jdm. auf die Nerven gehen
give a straight answer – eine klare Antwort geben
give sb. a hand to do sth. – jdm. helfen, etwas zu tun
give sb. a piece of one's mind – jdm. ungeschminkt sagen, was man meint
go off the deep end – aus der Haut fahren
go spare – völlig ausrasten
go to the dogs – vor die Hunde gehen

have a bee in one's bonnet – einen Tick haben
have a chip on one's shoulder – sich unfair behandelt/benachteiligt fühlen
have a close shave – einer Gefahr knapp entkommen
have a soft spot for sb. – eine Schwäche für jdn. haben
have egg on one's face – wie ein Depp dastehen
have one's back against the wall – in die Enge getrieben sein
have one's feet on the ground – eine handfeste Natur haben
have sb. over a barrel – jdn. in der Zange haben
have the gift of the gab – sehr redegewandt sein
hit it off with sb. – sich mit jdm. gut verstehen
hit the ceiling/roof – ausrasten

keep an eye on sb./sth. – ein Auge auf jdn./etwas haben
keep a straight face – ein ausdrucksloses Gesicht halten
keep one's fingers crossed – den Daumen drücken
keep one's hair on – ruhig bleiben
kick up a fuss – sich lauthals beschweren

leave sb. in the lurch – jdn. im Stich lassen
let the cat out of the bag – etwas preisgeben

make a go of sth. – etwas erfolgreich tun
make tracks – sich auf die Socken machen

pick a fight/quarrel with sb. – Streit mit jdm. anfangen
pick sb.'s brains – jdn. zum eigenen Vorteil ausfragen
play it safe – sichergehen
play sth. down – etwas verharmlosen
poke fun at sb./sth. – sich über jdn./etwas lustig machen
pour oil on troubled water – die Wogen glätten
pull sb. leg – jdn. auf den Arm nehmen
pull strings – etwas durch Beziehungen erreichen
pull the wool over sb.'s eyes – jdn. hinters Licht führen
put all one's eggs in one basket – alles auf eine Karte setzen
put the cart before the horse – eine Sache falsch herum betrachten
put the cat among the pigeons – für Unruhe sorgen
put sb.'s back up – jdn. verärgern
put sb. on the spot – jdn. in Verlegenheit bringen

screw sth. up – etwas vermasseln
see eye to eye with sb. – mit jdm. einverstanden sein
sell like hot cakes – wie warme Semmeln weggehen
sth. serves sb. right – etwas geschieht jdm. recht
smell a rat – Verdacht schöpfen

try to keep up with the Joneses – mit jdm. finanziell Schritt halten
turn a blind eye to sth. – etwas bewusst ignorieren
not turn a hair – nicht mit der Wimper zucken
turn sb./sth.down – jdm./etwas ablehnen

wash one's hands of sb./sth. – mit jdm./etwas nichts mehr zu tun haben wollen

Falsche Freunde

Als „falsche Freunde" bezeichnet man jene englischen Wörter, die deutschen Wörtern sehr ähneln, aber etwas ganz anderes bedeuten. Es ist verlockend, „brav" mit *brave* und „Chef" mit *chef* zu übersetzen. Es ist aber leider falsch und für den Englischsprachigen zudem völlig unverständlich.

In den folgenden Einträgen steht zuerst das deutsche Ausgangswort mit einem Beispielsatz und seiner Übersetzung mit dem ***richtigen*** englischen Begriff. Dann folgt ein Satz, in dem der *falsche Freund* verwendet wird.

Akademiker/in
Alle Ärzte sind Akademiker.
*All doctors are **graduates.***

Academics teach and do research at universities.
Gelehrte lehren und forschen an Hochschulen.

aktuell
Arbeitslosigkeit ist das wichtigste aktuelle Thema.
*Unemployment is the most important **current** topic.*

He actually said the precise opposite.
Tatsächlich sagte er das genaue Gegenteil.

bekommen
Heute habe ich über 20 E-Mails bekommen.
*I **got/received** over 20 emails today.*

Our boss always becomes angry if you question his decisions.
Unser Chef wird immer ärgerlich, wenn man seine Entscheidungen infrage stellt.

sich blamieren
Die Mannschaft hat sich blamiert.
*The team made a **fool of itself.***

The trainer blamed the referee.
Der Trainer gab dem Schiedsrichter die Schuld.

brav
Mein Hund ist sehr brav.
My dog is ***very good.***

Are you brave enough to demand better pay?
Bist du mutig genug, eine bessere Bezahlung zu verlangen?

Chef
Mein Chef ist häufig geschäftlich verreist.
My ***boss*** *is often away on business.*

The chef here has won a lot of prizes.
Der Koch hier hat viele Preise gewonnen.

desinteressiert
Im Moment ist Markus völlig desinteressiert.
At the moment, Markus is completely ***uninterested.***

Sport commentators should be disinterested observers.
Sportkommentatoren sollten unparteiische Beobachter sein.

dezent
Kannst du nicht dezentere Kleidung tragen?
Can't you wear ***more restrained*** *clothes?*

John is a thoroughly decent man.
John ist ein durch und durch anständiger Mann.

eventuell
Eventuell sehen wir uns am Wochenende.
Maybe *we'll see each other at the weekend.*

The plane eventually took off.
Schließlich hob das Flugzeug ab.

irritieren
Lass dich nicht durch sein merkwürdiges Benehmen irritieren.
Don't be ***confused/put off*** *by his strange behaviour.*

Ben irritated Anna a lot with his endless phone calls.
Ben hat Ann mit seinen endlosen Telefonanrufen sehr verärgert.

komfortabel
Das neue Betriebssystem ist äußerst komfortabel.
The new operating system is extremely ***convenient.***

Is that hard chair comfortable enough?
Ist der harte Stuhl bequem genug?

konsequent
Bei der Hundedressur muss man absolut konsequent sein.
You must be absolutely ***consistent*** *when training dogs.*

Consequently, I have no other choice.
Folglich habe ich keine andere Wahl.

meinen
Was meinst du dazu?
What do you ***think*** *about it?*

What does 'to evade' mean in German?
Was bedeutet „*to evade*" auf Deutsch?

miserabel
Dieses Essen ist absolut miserabel.
This meal is absolutely ***awful.***

Mozart died a miserable death.
Mozart starb einen elenden Tod.

Notiz
Bei Verkaufsgesprächen sollte man sich immer Notizen machen.
You should always take ***notes*** *at sales meetings.*

The notice says the shop is closed.
Auf dem Aushang steht, dass das Geschäft geschlossen ist.

Rente
Viele junge Leute sparen nichts für ihre Rente.
*A lot of young people save nothing for their **pension.***

They haven't paid their rent for months.
Sie haben seit Monaten ihre Miete nicht bezahlt.

Rezept
Der Arzt gab mir ein Rezept gegen Schlaflosigkeit.
*The doctor gave me a **prescription** for insomnia.*

Have you tried this Italian recipe yet?
Hast du dieses italienische Rezept schon ausprobiert?

sensibel
Bei solchen Sachen kann Beate sehr sensibel sein.
*Beate can be very **sensitive** about such things.*

The only sensible thing to do with spam is to delete it.
Die einzig vernünftige Verfahrensweise mit Spam ist, es zu löschen.

seriös
Einige Verkäufer sind nicht ganz seriös.
*Some salesmen are not quite **trustworthy/reputable.***

Is terrorism really a serious danger?
Ist der Terrorismus wirklich eine ernste Gefahr?

spenden
Er spendet viel Geld für wohltätige Zwecke.
*He **donates/gives** a lot of money to charity.*

Ben shouldn't spend so much money on cars.
Ben sollte nicht so viel Geld für Autos ausgeben.

sympathisch, Sympathie
Lisa ist eine sehr sympathische Frau.
*Lisa is a very **pleasant/likeable** woman.*

Doctors show little sympathy for smokers.
Ärzte zeigen wenig Mitgefühl für Raucher.

übersehen
Der Autofahrer hat den Fahrradfahrer völlig übersehen.
*The car driver completely **overlooked** the cyclist.*

Two security men oversee the car park at night.
Nachts überwachen zwei Sicherheitsmänner den Parkplatz.

Unternehmer/in
Ohne Unternehmerinnen und Unternehmer gäbe es viel weniger Arbeitsplätze.
*Without **entrepreneurs** there would be far fewer jobs.*

Undertakers are people who arrange funerals.
Leichenbestatter sind Menschen, die Beerdigungen arrangieren.

So klappt's in der 10. Klasse

Prüfungswissen Deutsch
10. Klasse
Schülerbuch mit Lerntipps,
Tests und Lösungen

Gymnasium
128 Seiten mit Abb.,
Paperback
ISBN 978-3-589-22622-1

Realschule
128 Seiten mit Abb.,
Paperback
ISBN 978-3-589-22621-4

Prüfungswissen Englisch
10. Klasse
Schülerbuch mit Lerntipps,
Tests und Lösungen

Gymnasium
128 Seiten mit Abb.,
Paperback
ISBN 978-3-589-22624-5

Realschule
120 Seiten mit Abb.,
Paperback
ISBN 978-3-589-22623-8

Prüfungswissen Mathematik
10. Klasse
Schülerbuch mit Lerntipps,
Tests und Lösungen

Gymnasium
128 Seiten mit Abb.,
Paperback
ISBN 978-3-589-22626-9

Realschule
128 Seiten mit Abb.,
Paperback
ISBN 978-3-589-22625-2

Informieren Sie sich unter der Nummer 0180 12 120 20 (3,9 ct/min. aus dem Festnetz der Dt. Telekom) oder in unserem Onlineshop: www.cornelsen-shop.de

Cornelsen
SCRIPTOR